Hopper Drawings

44 Works by Edward Hopper

From the Permanent Collection of the
Whitney Museum of American Art

DOVER PUBLICATIONS, INC., NEW YORK

Photography credits, cover and pp. 2, 11, 31, 33, 38: Geoffrey Clements.

Hopper Drawings: 44 Works from the Permanent Collection of the Whitney Museum of American Art
is a new work, first published by Dover Publications, Inc., in 1989.

Manufactured in the United States of America
Dover Publications, Inc.
31 East 2nd Street
Mineola, N.Y. 11501

Library of Congress Cataloging-in-Publication Data

Hopper, Edward, 1882–1967.
Hopper drawings.

"From the permanent collection of the Whitney Museum of American Art."
1. Hopper, Edward, 1882–1967—Catalogs.
2. Artists' preparatory studies—United States—Catalogs.
3. Drawing—New York (N.Y.)—Catalogs.
4. Whitney Museum of American Art—Catalogs.
I. Whitney Museum of American Art. II. Title.
NC139.H65A4 1989 741'.973 88-30951
ISBN 0-486-25854-8

Introduction

Edward Hopper (1882–1967), premier American realist, painted the stark and lonely places of twentieth-century America, evoking in these paintings an elusive mood of longing and half-dread, a sensation of opportunities missed, of lives wasted. Hopper's drawings are in large part preliminary sketches for his paintings, and while the most polished of these yield some of this mood, most are not quite so evocative. Hopper's studies, in fact, serve simply to record those elements—qualities of light, compositional arrangements, the posture of the figure—that he would call upon to create such a mood. They are working drawings—no-nonsense, practical drawings. Words suffice, for example, as clues to the colors and particular light Hopper wants for his painting—"warm roof," "blue gray shadow," written on a drawing for *Route 6, Eastham* (p. 38). As Hopper explained to Lloyd Goodrich, former director of the Whitney Museum of American Art, if he finished his drawings too much, or if he made color sketches, he might end up merely copying them onto canvas rather than calling upon "the concept in his mind." The final synthesis of all the elements, along with the undefinable energy that unites and animates them, await the finished canvas.

Not all of Hopper's drawings, however, were guided by such pragmatism. In his independent sheets, his love of both drawing materials and the subject itself comes through in richly black, rugged landscape renderings (pp. 42 and 43) or in sultry images of student days in Paris (p. 3). Hopper's emotional life is sometimes revealed even in his utilitarian preparatory studies, especially those of his wife, Josephine Nivison Hopper, who served as his model. She seems, for example, tentative, weary or frightened in a drawing for *Morning Sun* (p. 21) and, in a study for *Girlie Show* (p. 26), much more vulnerable than the steely blonde she becomes in the final painting. Hopper's many drawn portraits of Jo represent a poignant study of their relationship: she appears playful and alluring, domestic and comforting, withdrawn and introspective (pp. 5, 8–10).

In one remarkable series of drawings done at the Whitney Studio Club in the early twenties (pp. 12–20), Hopper rendered the figure as he never would again, glorifying the flesh-and-blood quality of his models. Thickly drawn and smudged, or linear and lightly sketched, these studies are celebrations of the nude by a relatively young artist. Later, in his paintings, he would reject the sensuality of the figure in favor of generalized, blocky forms that relate almost architectonically to their spare settings. Hopper ended his sketching sessions at the club in 1924—a decision no doubt prompted by the often jealous and vocal Jo, whom he married that year. She would thereafter become his only model, and it was perhaps in an effort at appeasement that he inscribed many of these drawings to her.

Hopper's drawings are represented in abundance in the collection of the Whitney Museum of American Art. By virtue of the generous bequest of Josephine Hopper, in 1970 the Whitney Museum became the largest repository of Hopper's art. The works in the bequest span his entire career, from childhood musings to mature, finished paintings, and include thousands of drawings. The enormous task of cataloging and researching the drawings was begun by Lloyd Goodrich with Elizabeth Tweedy Streibert and continued by Dr. Gail Levin. It is hoped that one day the Whitney Museum will have a study center which will allow scholars greater access to these works. They constitute a unique treasury that continues to enrich and develop our understanding of this major American artist.

Deborah Lyons
Advisor, Hopper Collection
Whitney Museum of American Art

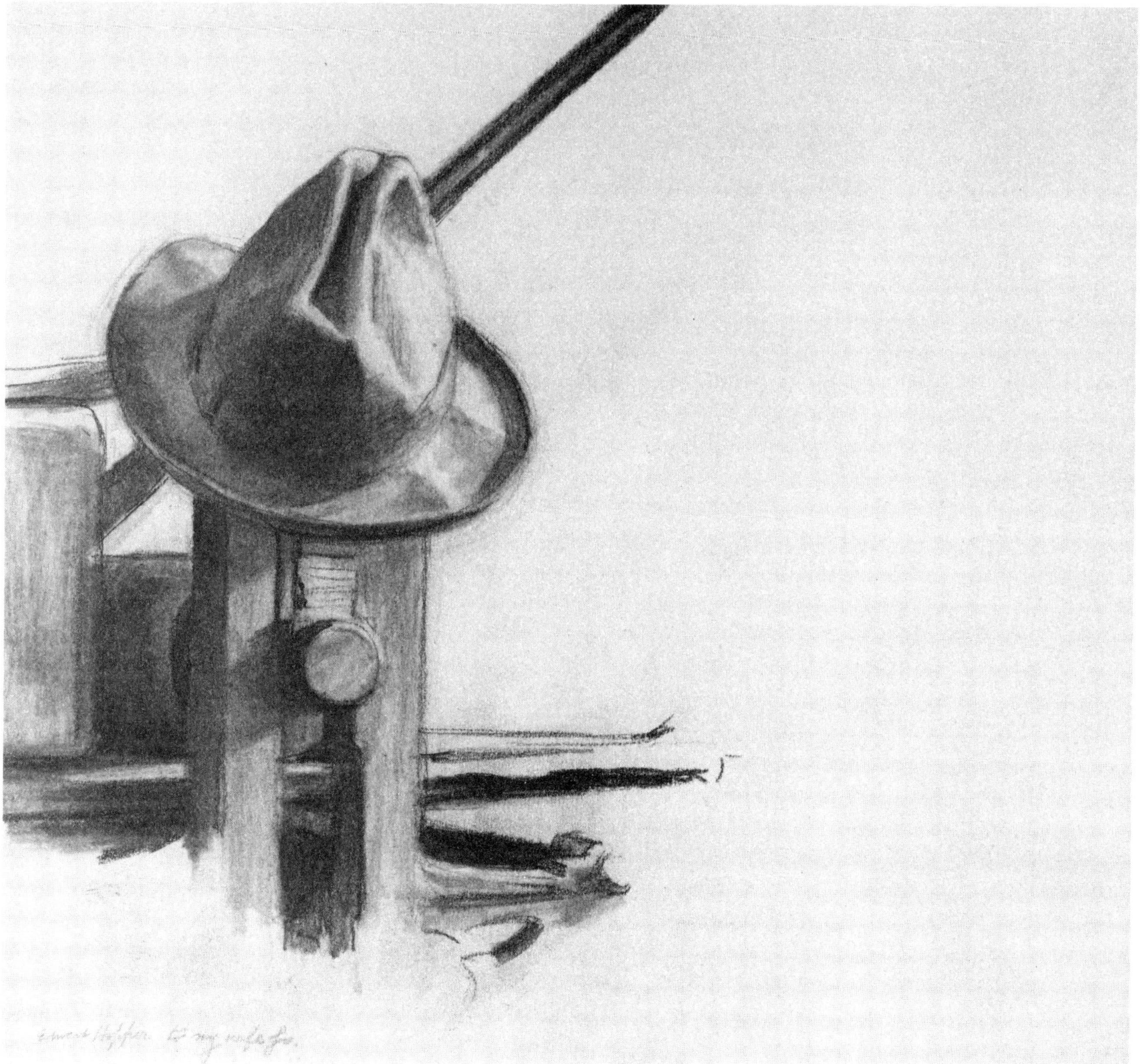

Hopper's Hat on His Etching Press, n.d.
Conté on paper, 11⅛ × 15¼ inches. Josephine N. Hopper Bequest   70.344

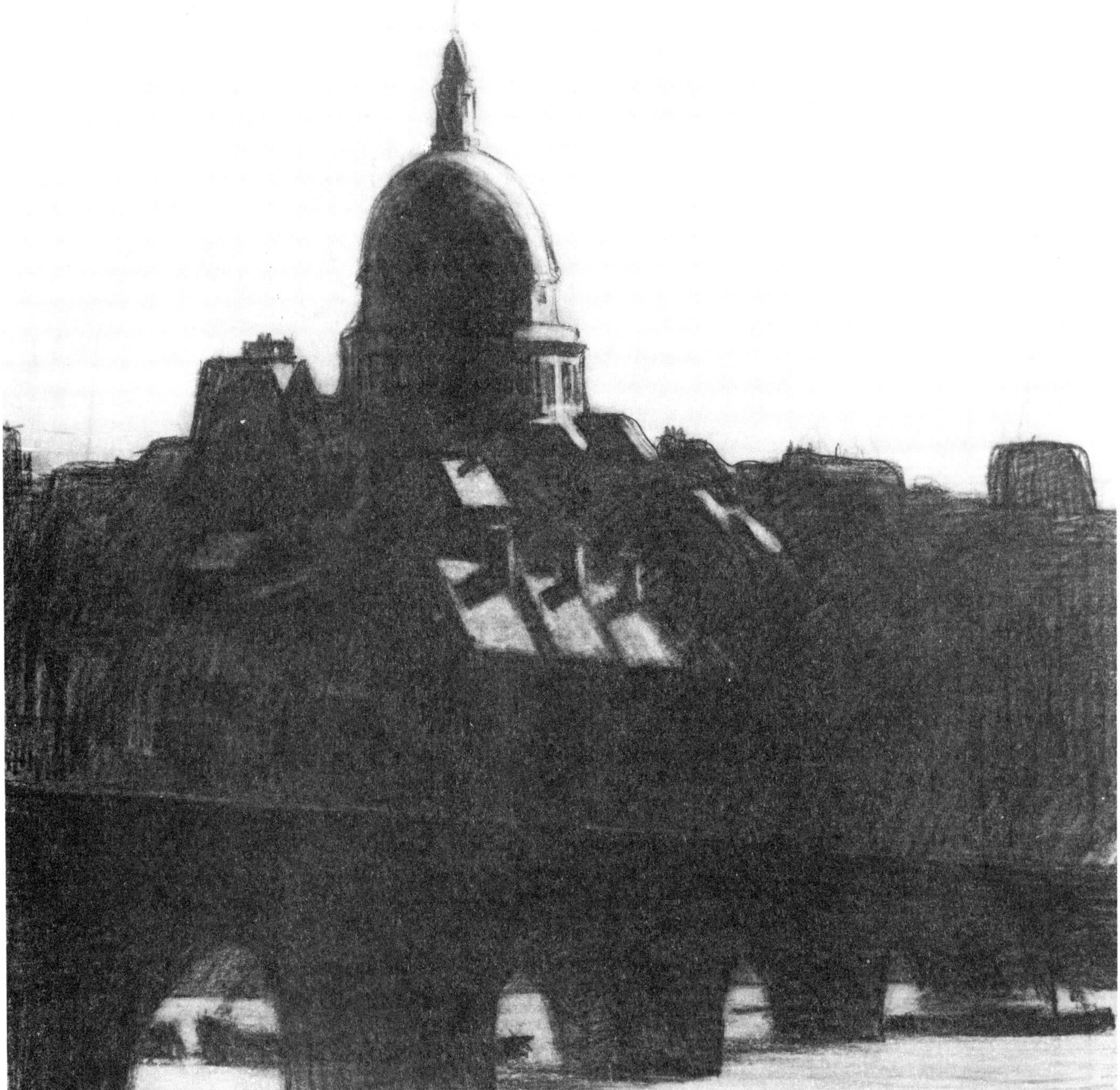

Dome, 1906–07 or 1909
Conté, wash, charcoal and pencil on paper, 21⅜ × 19⅞ inches.
Josephine N. Hopper Bequest 70.1434

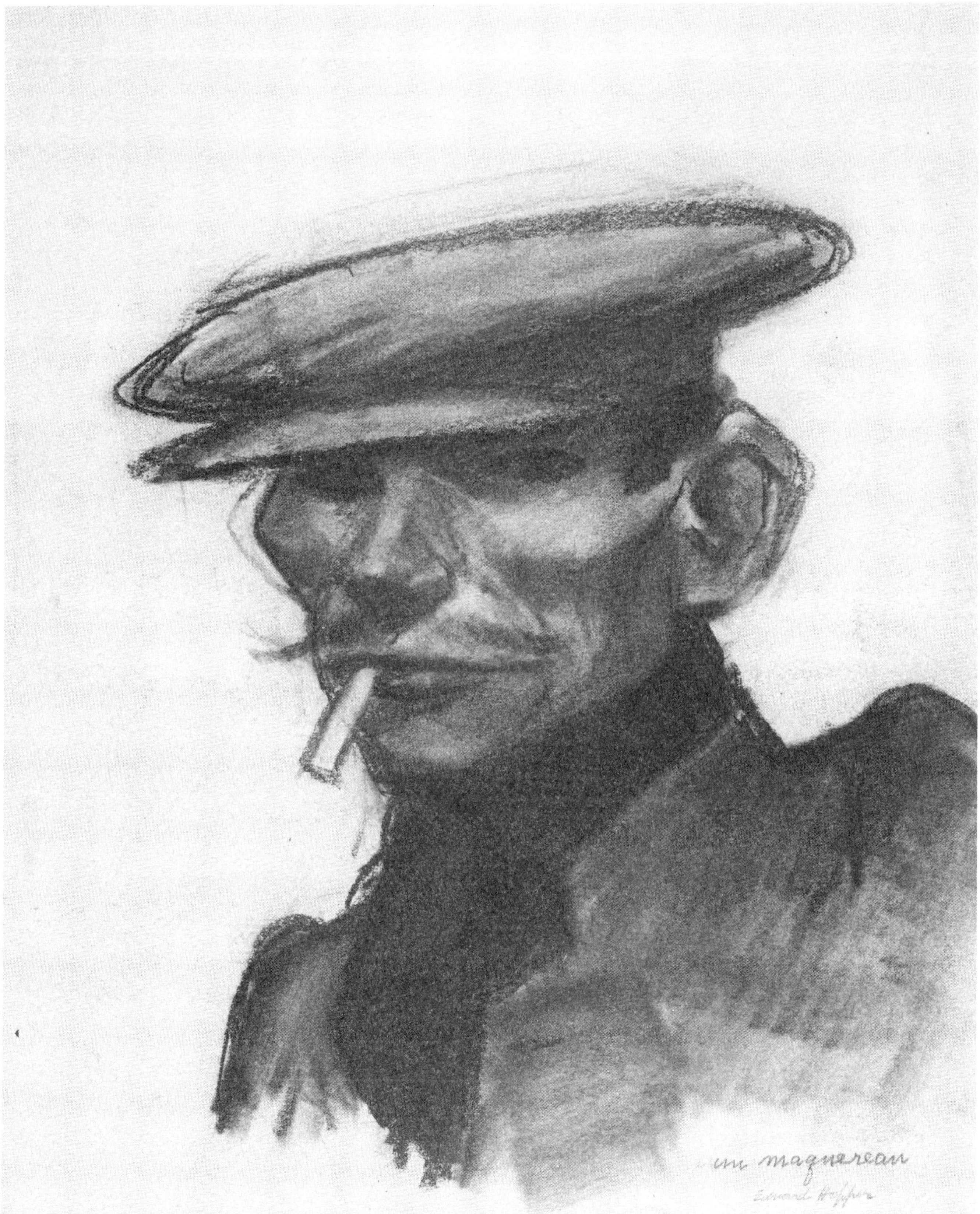

Un Maquereau (study for *Soir Bleu*), 1914
Conté on paper, 10 × 8⅜ inches. Josephine N. Hopper Bequest 70.318

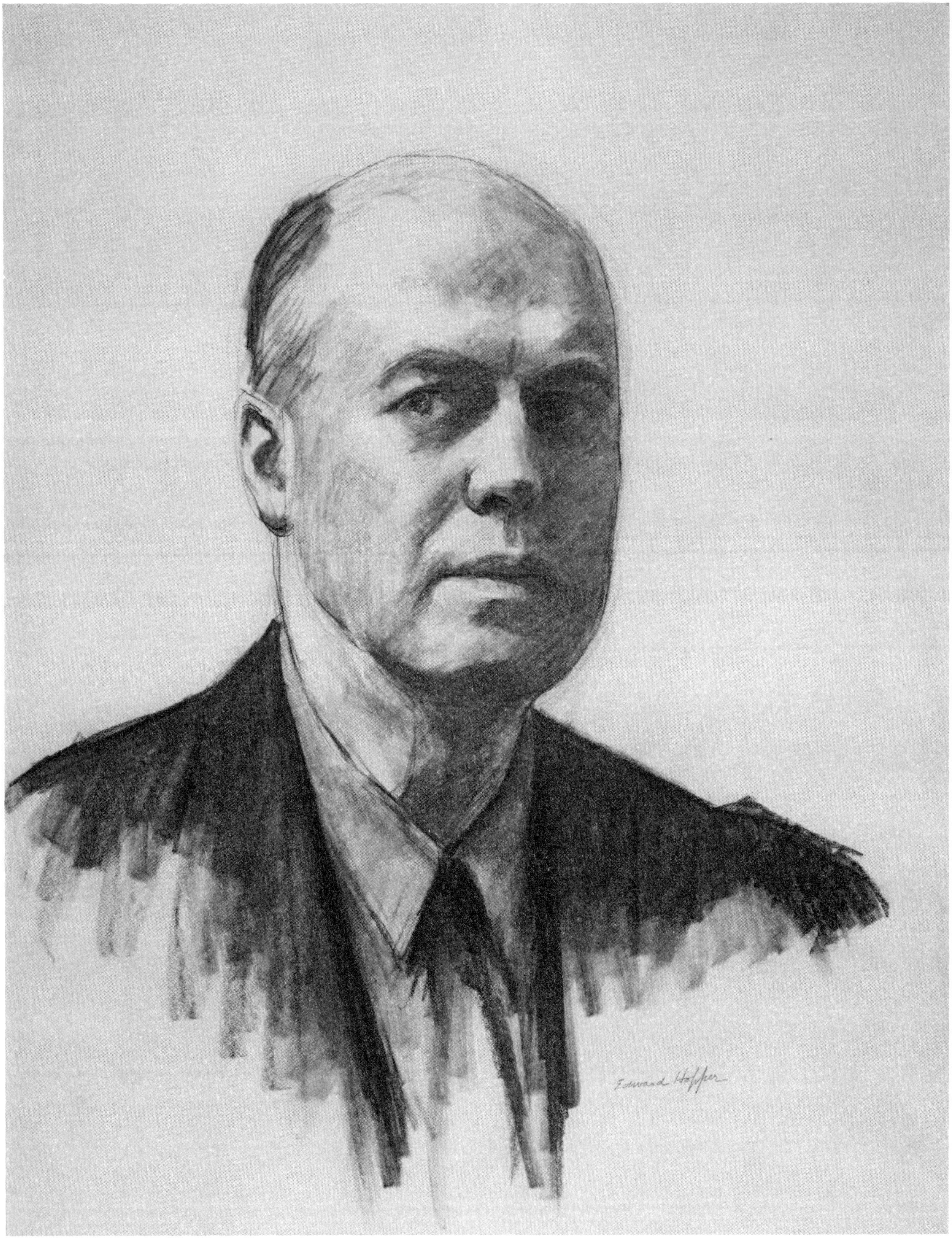

Self-Portrait, 1945
Conté on paper, 22 × 15 inches. Josephine N. Hopper Bequest 70.287

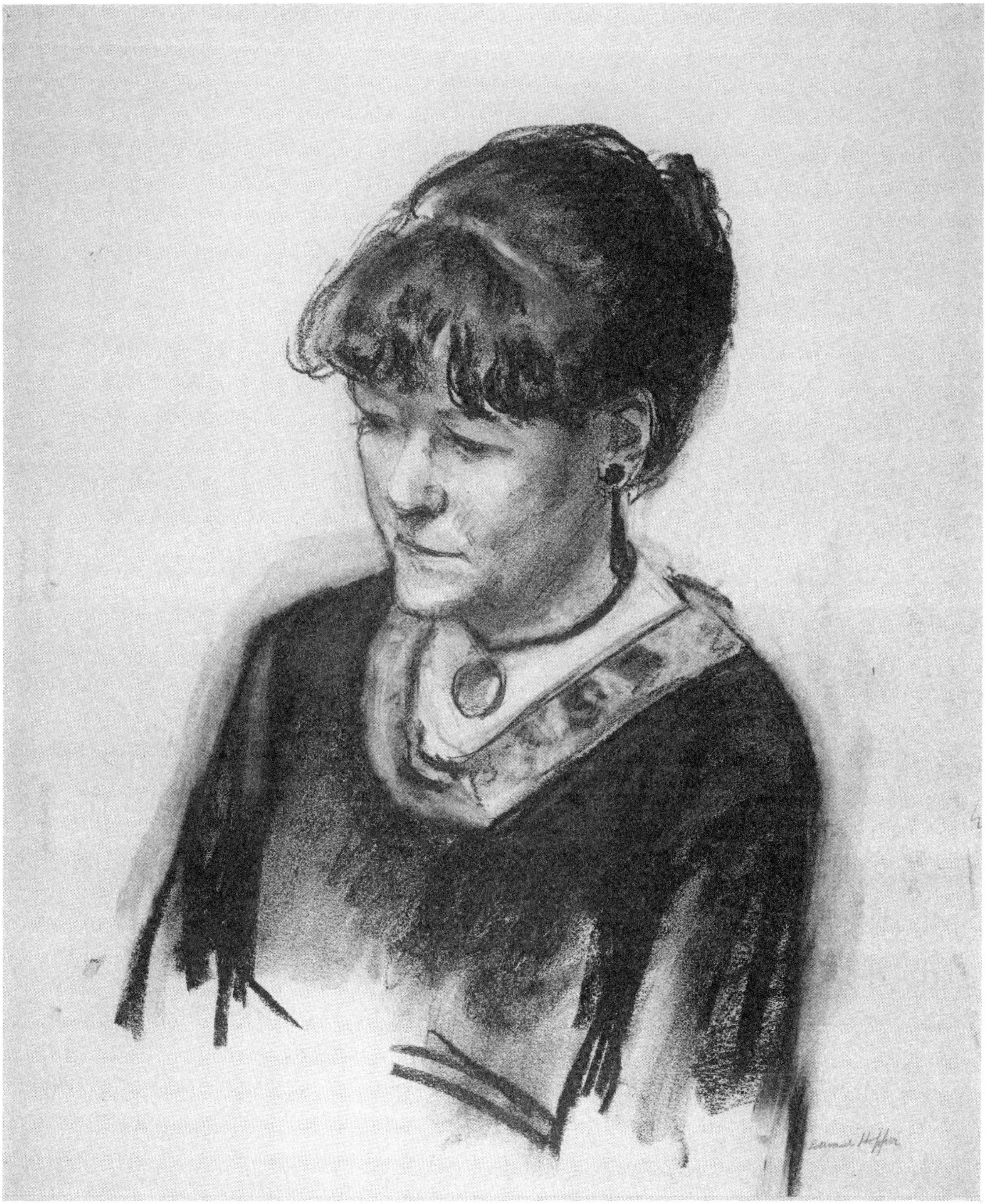

Jo Hopper, 1945–50
Charcoal on paper, 18 × 15½ inches. Josephine N. Hopper Bequest 70.288

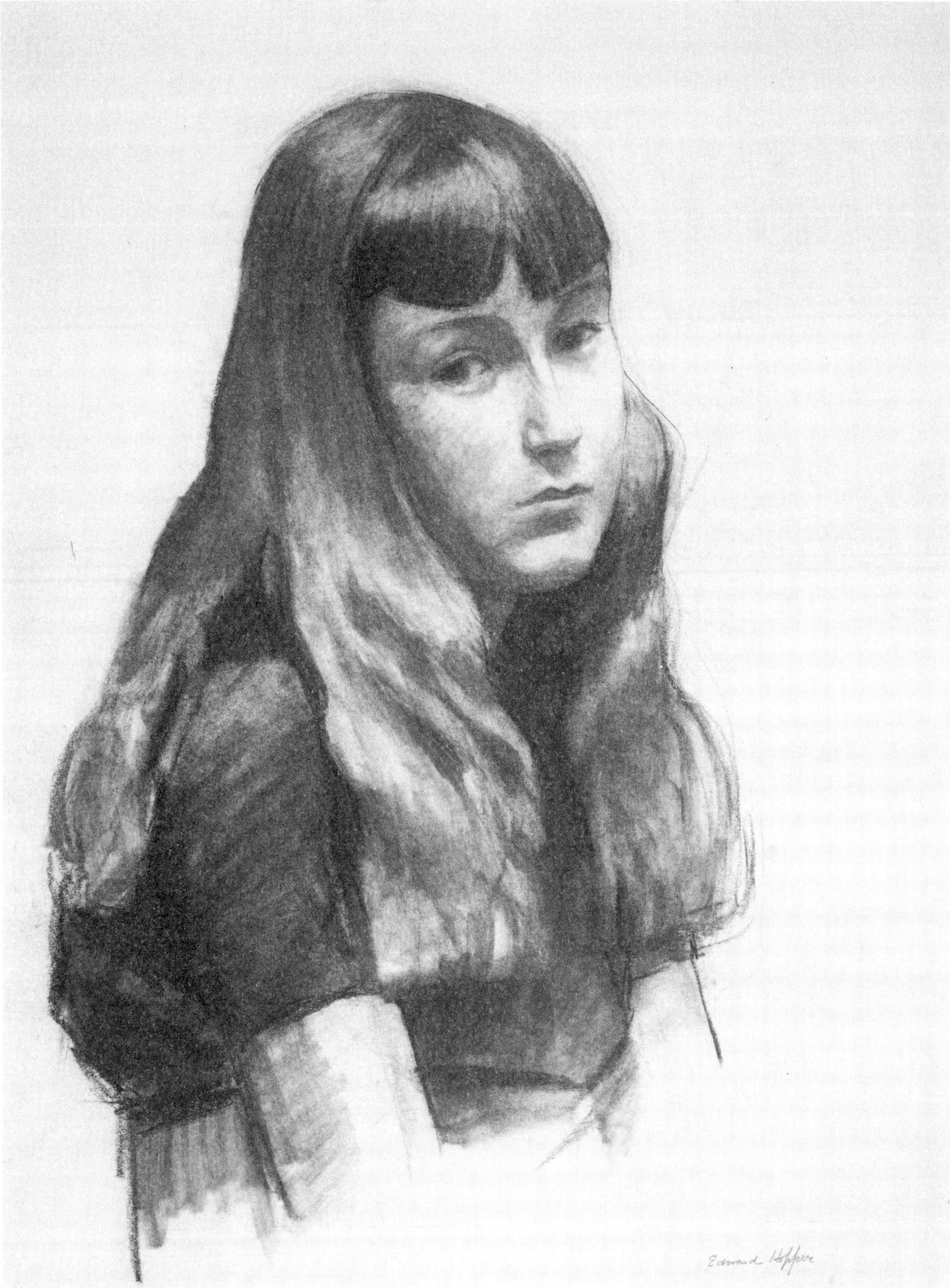

Portrait of Stella Falkner, c. 1936–38
Sanguine on paper, 21 × 16¼ inches. Josephine N. Hopper Bequest 70.908

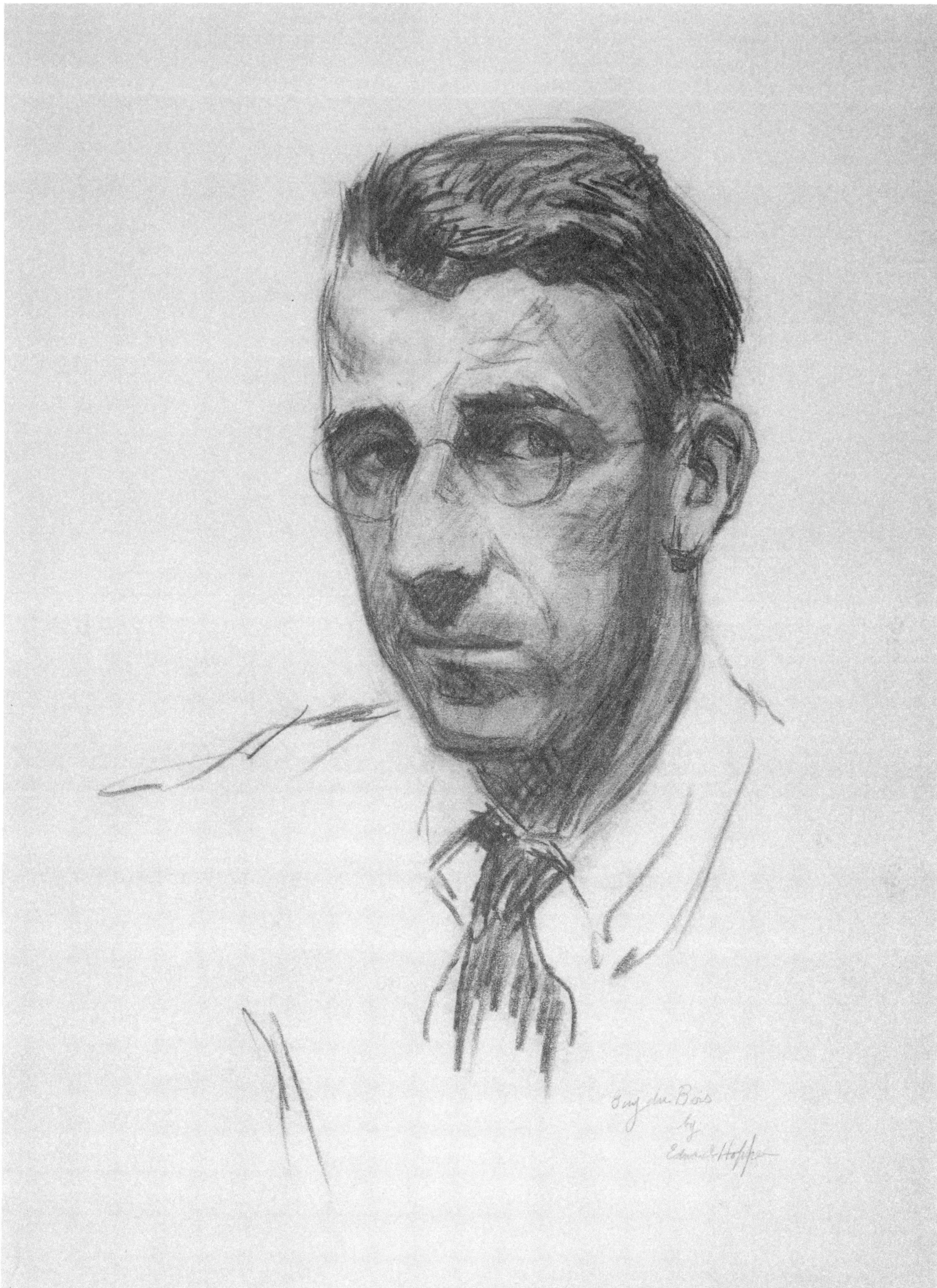

Portrait of Guy Pène du Bois, 1919
Sanguine on paper, 21 × 16 inches. Josephine N. Hopper Bequest 70.907

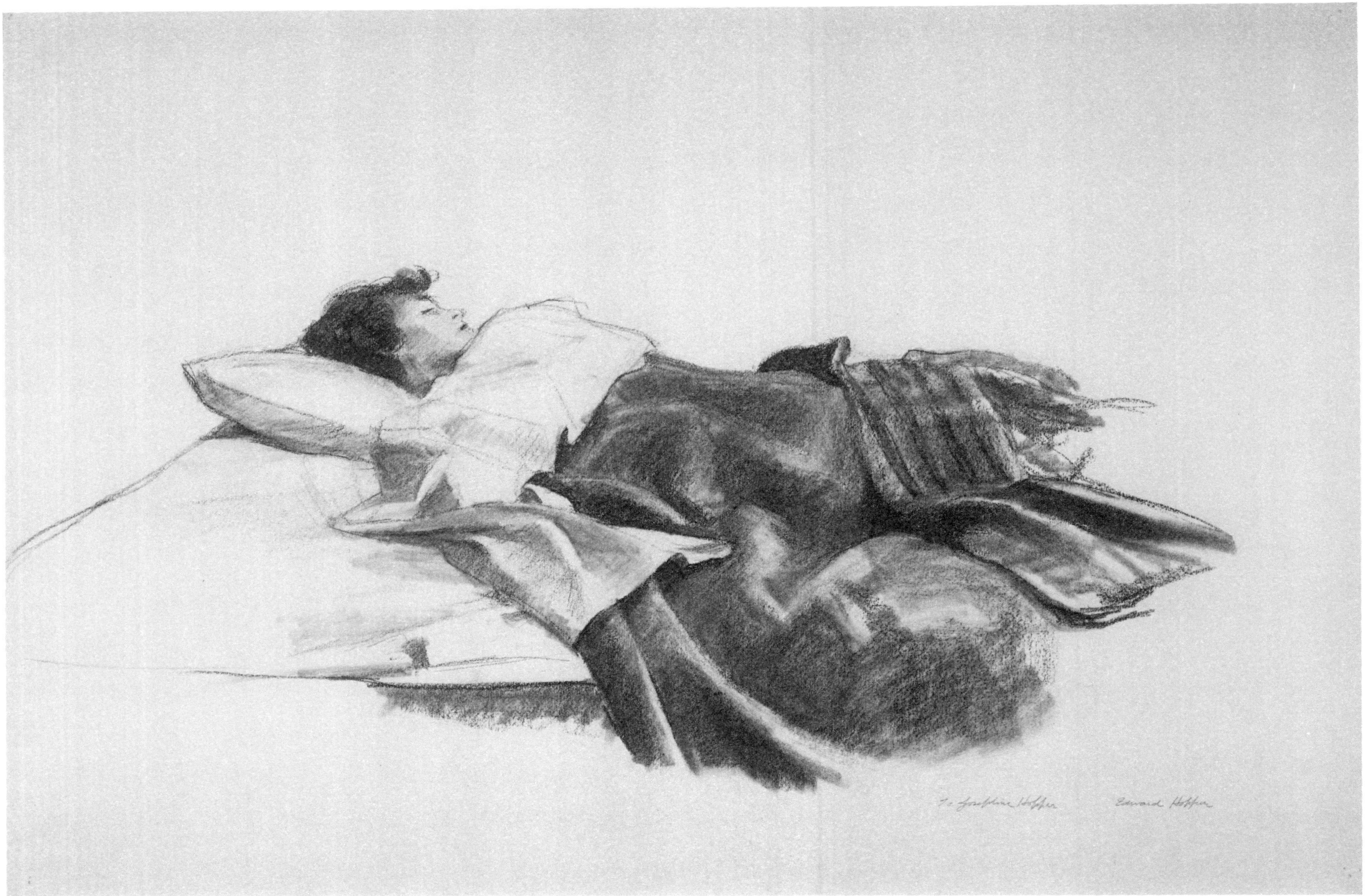

Jo Sleeping, 1940–45
Conté on paper, 15 × 22⅛ inches. Josephine N. Hopper Bequest   70.292

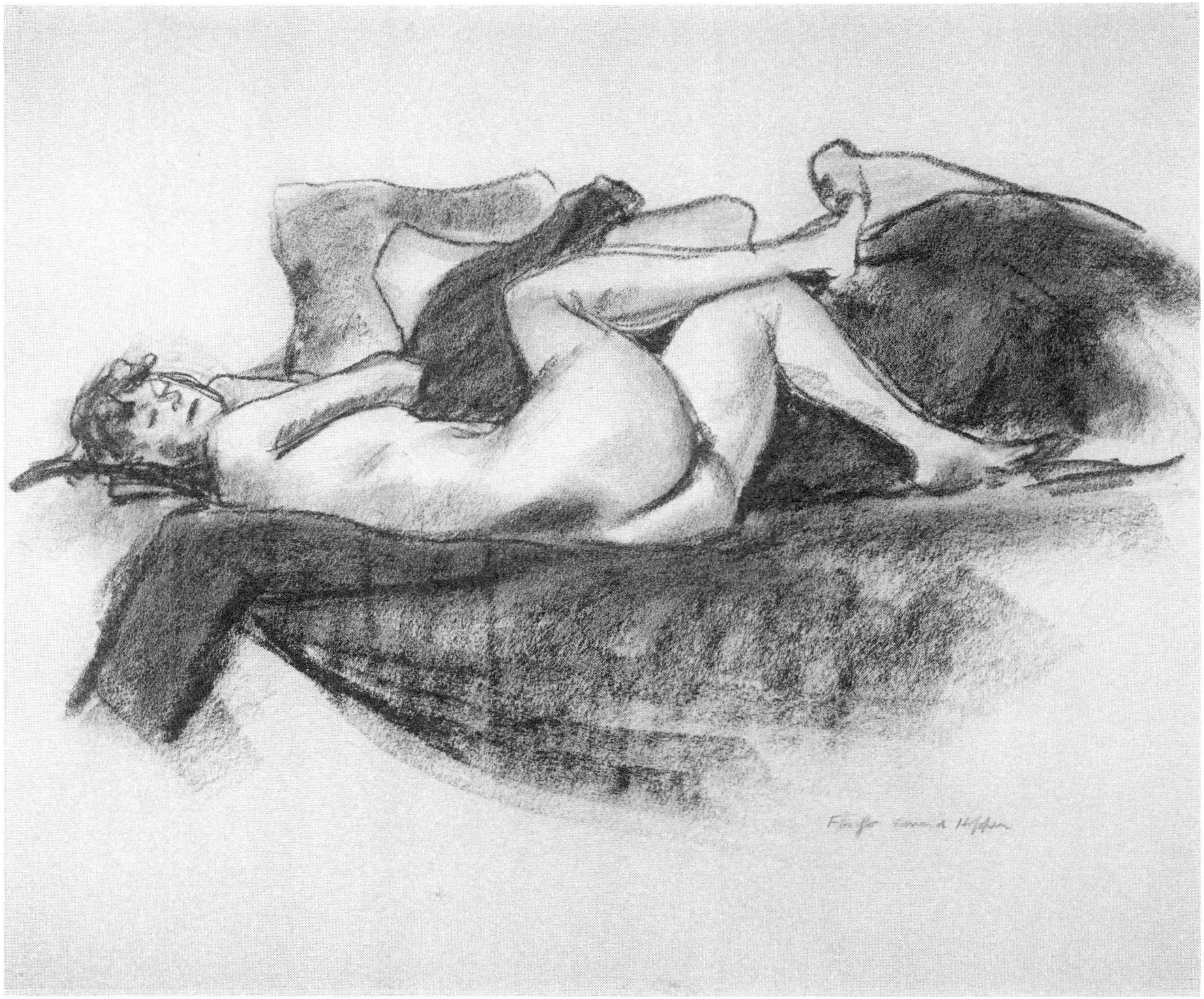

Jo Hopper Reclining on a Couch, 1925–30
Charcoal on paper, 15⅝ × 18 inches. Josephine N. Hopper Bequest 70.296

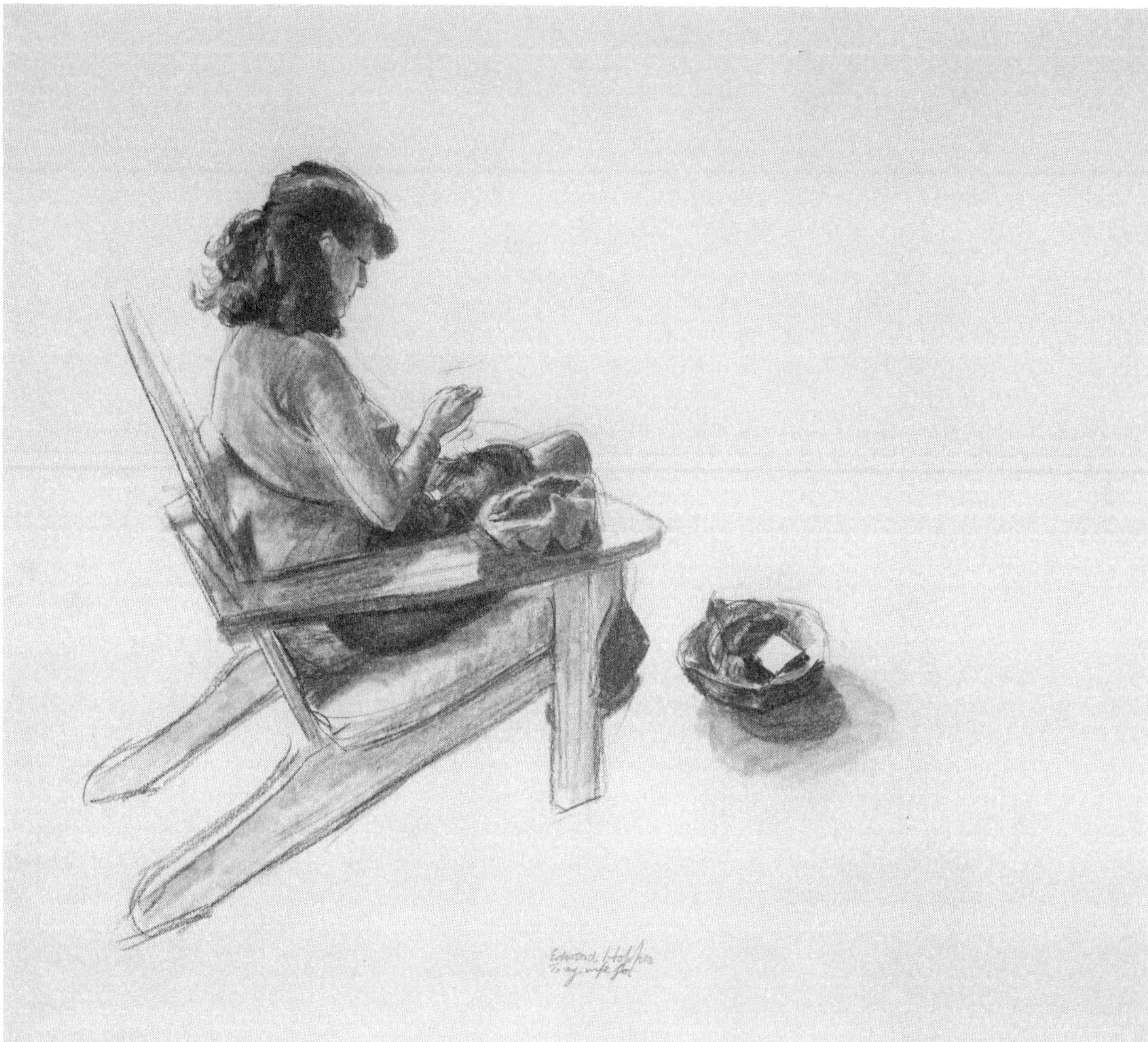

Jo Hopper, 1934–40
Conté on paper, 15 × 19 inches. Josephine N. Hopper Bequest 70.289

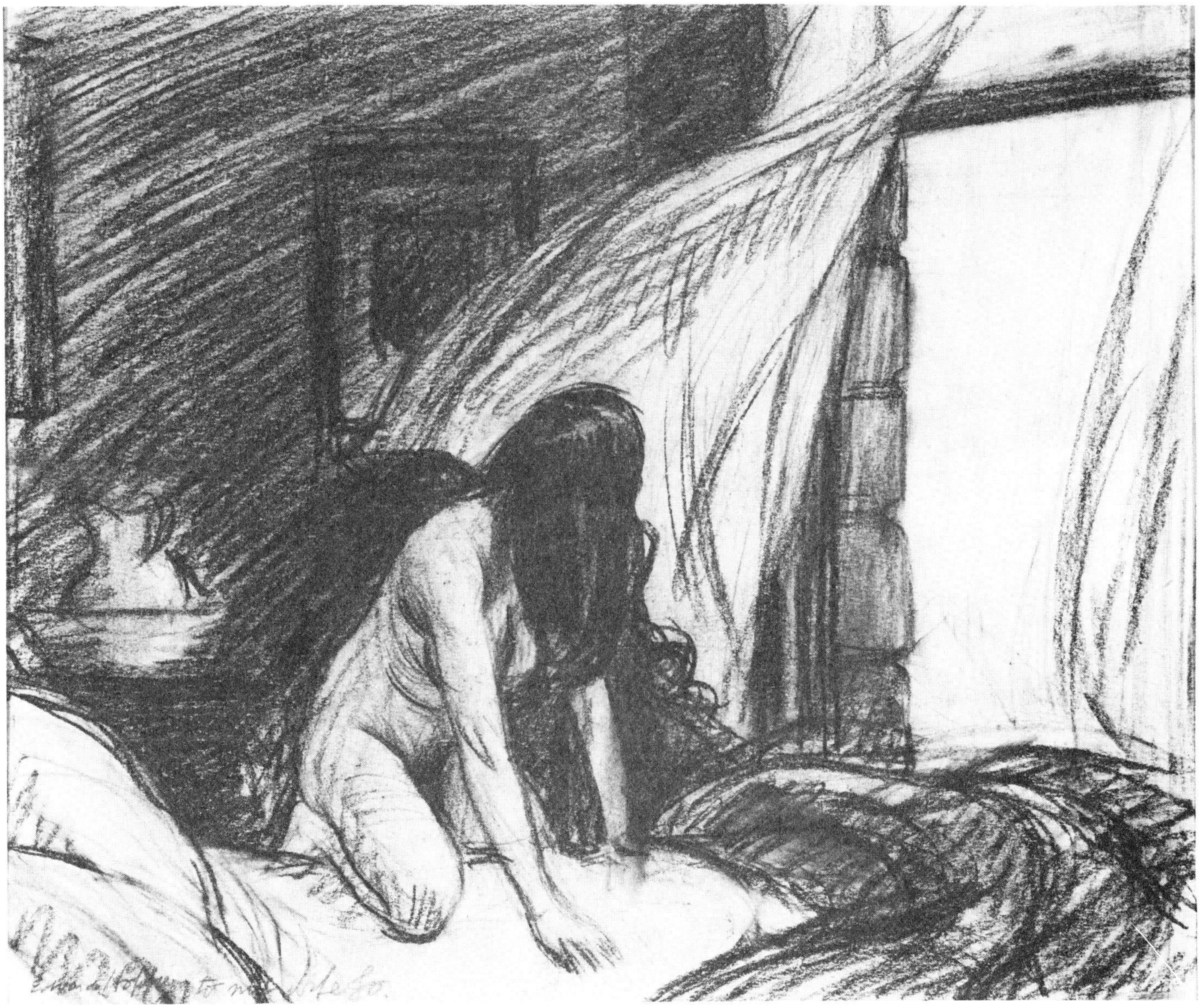

Study for *Evening Wind*, 1921
Conté and charcoal on paper, 10 × 13 15/16 inches.
Josephine N. Hopper Bequest 70.343

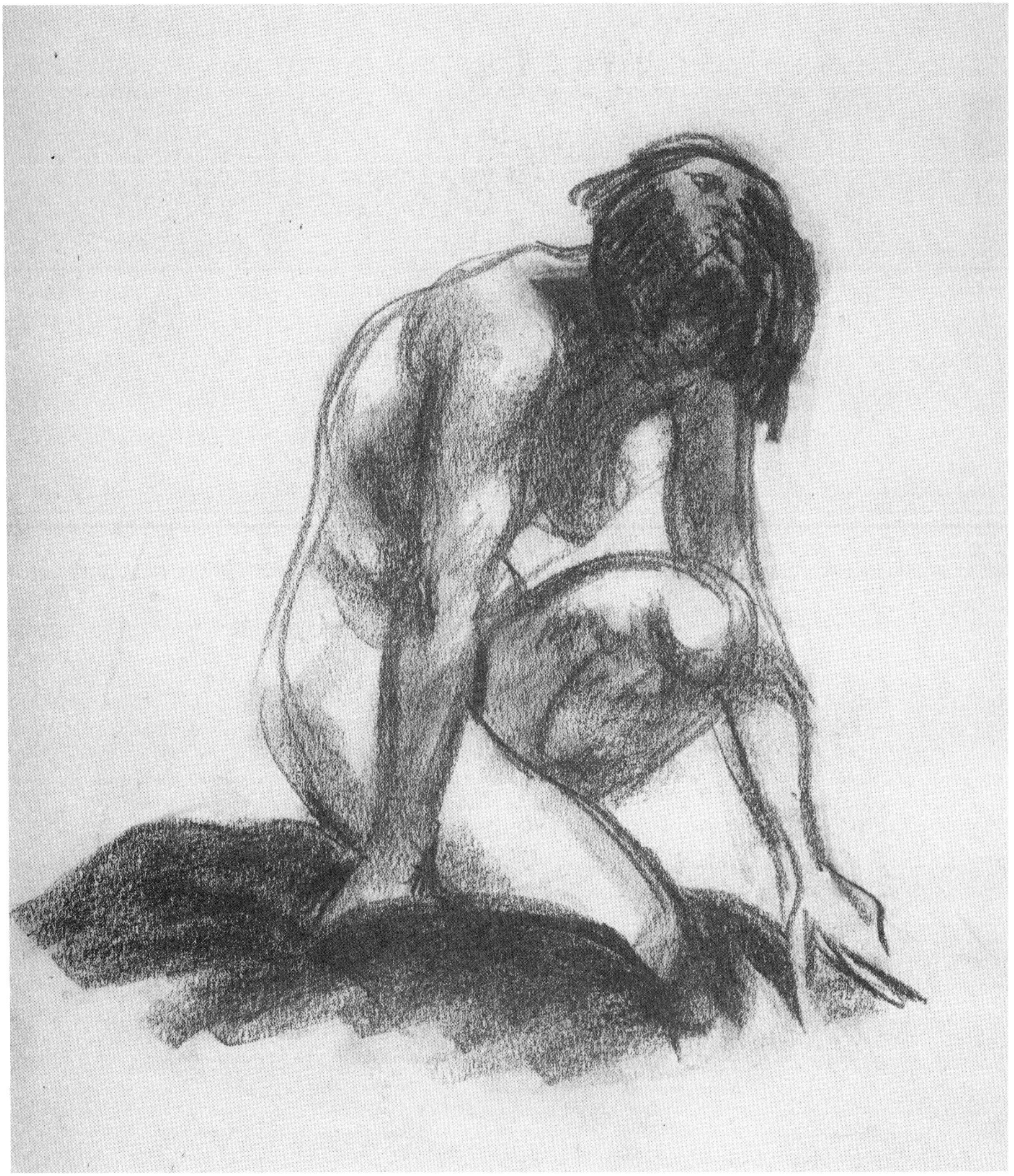

Kneeling Nude, c. 1923–24
Sanguine on paper, 17 15/16 × 11½ inches. Josephine N. Hopper Bequest 70.548

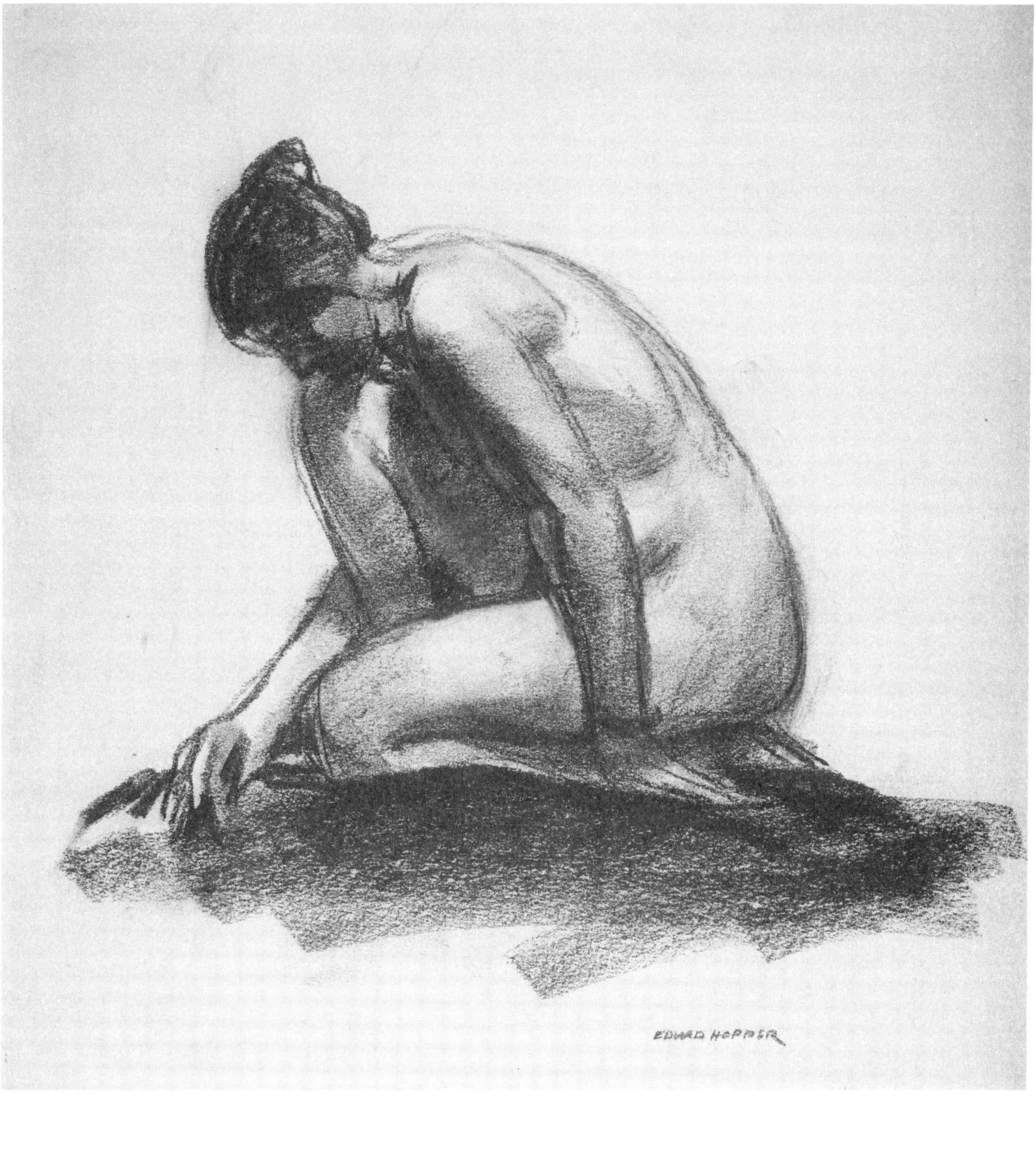

Kneeling Nude, c. 1923–24
Sanguine on paper, 18 15/16 × 11 7/8 inches. Josephine N. Hopper Bequest 70.945

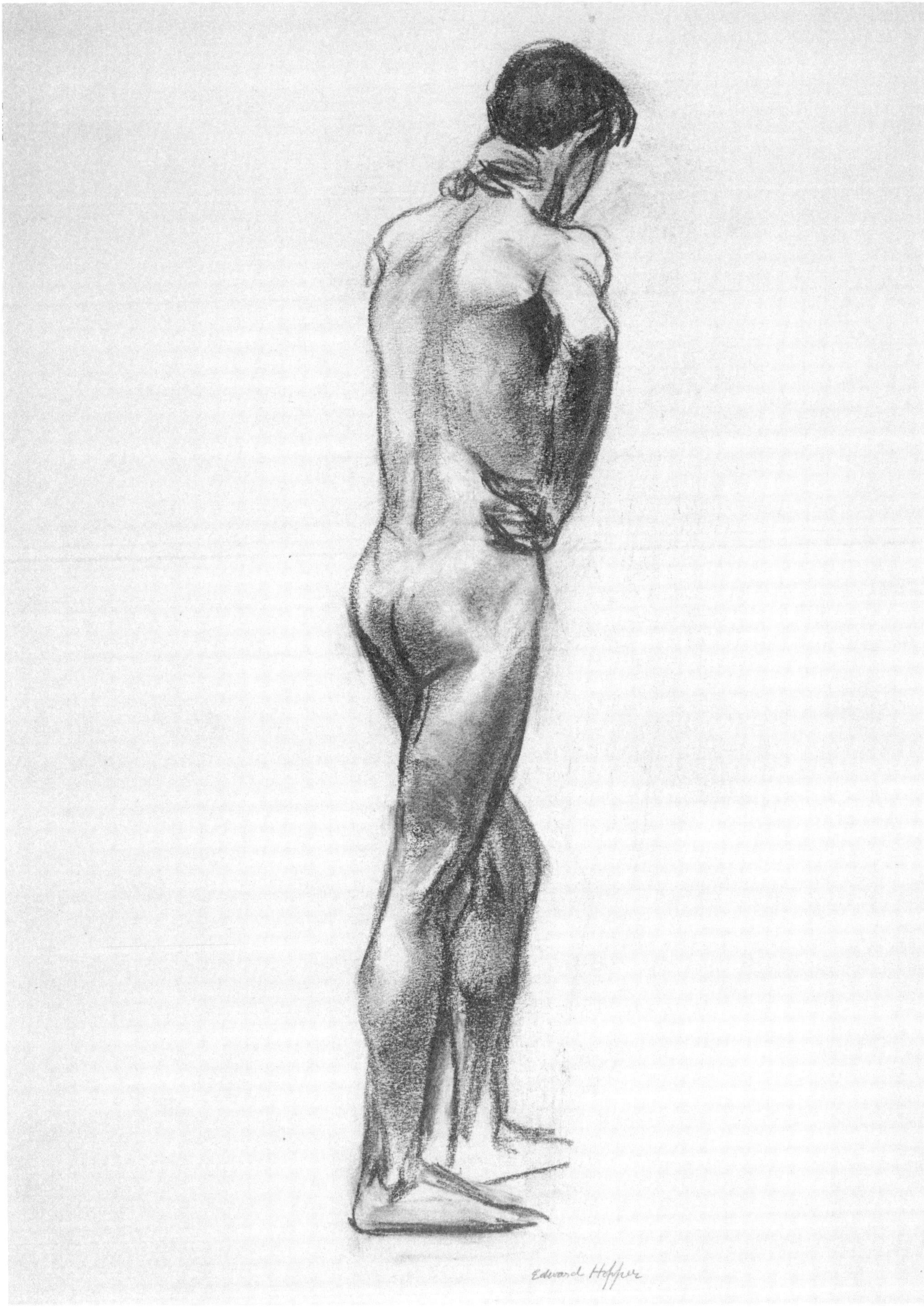

Standing Male Nude, Rear, c. 1923–24
Sanguine on paper, 22 1/16 × 15 1/16 inches. Josephine N. Hopper Bequest 70.691

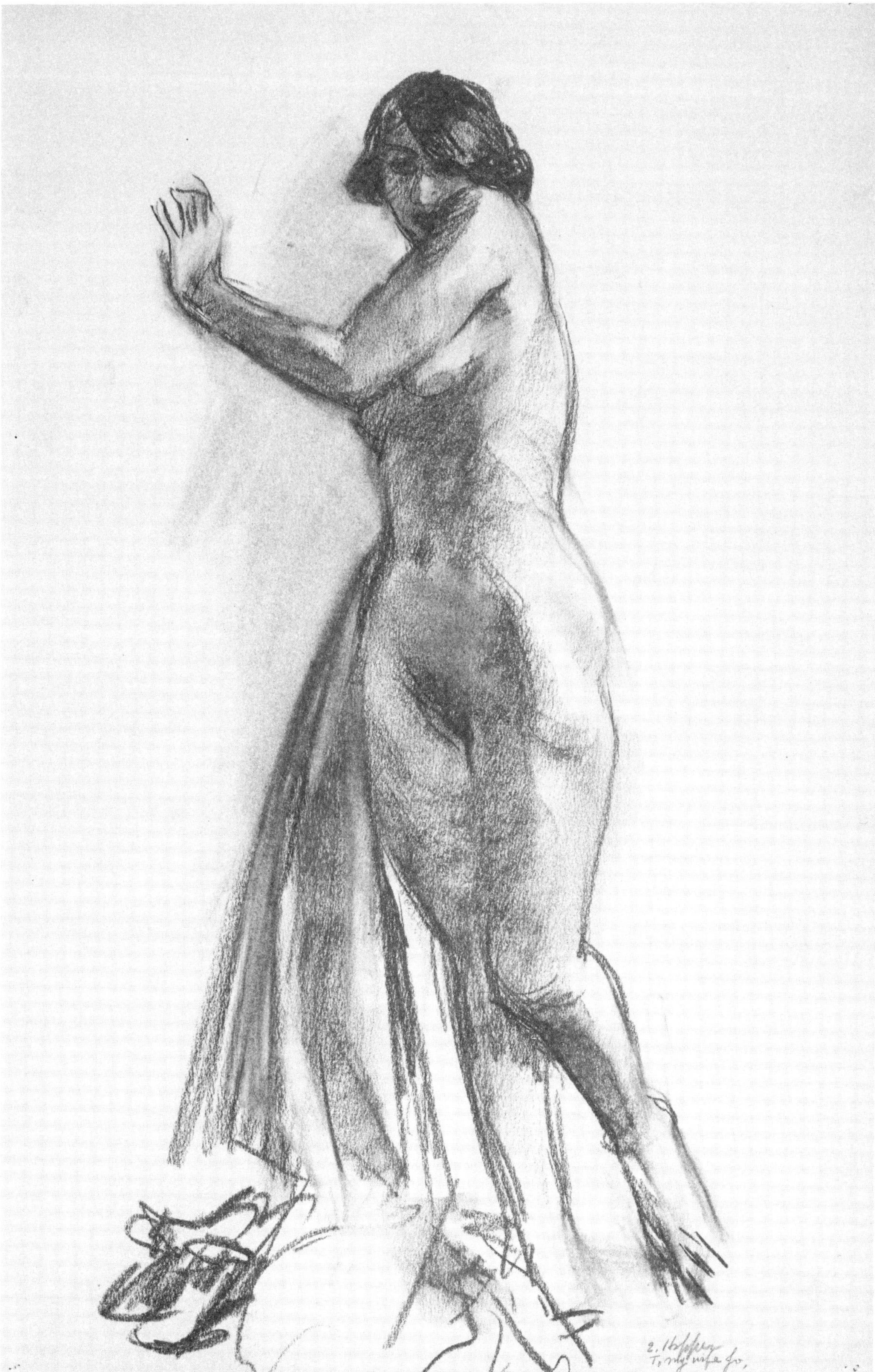

Standing Nude with Drape, c. 1923–24
Conté on paper, 17 15/16 × 11½ inches. Josephine N. Hopper Bequest 70.667

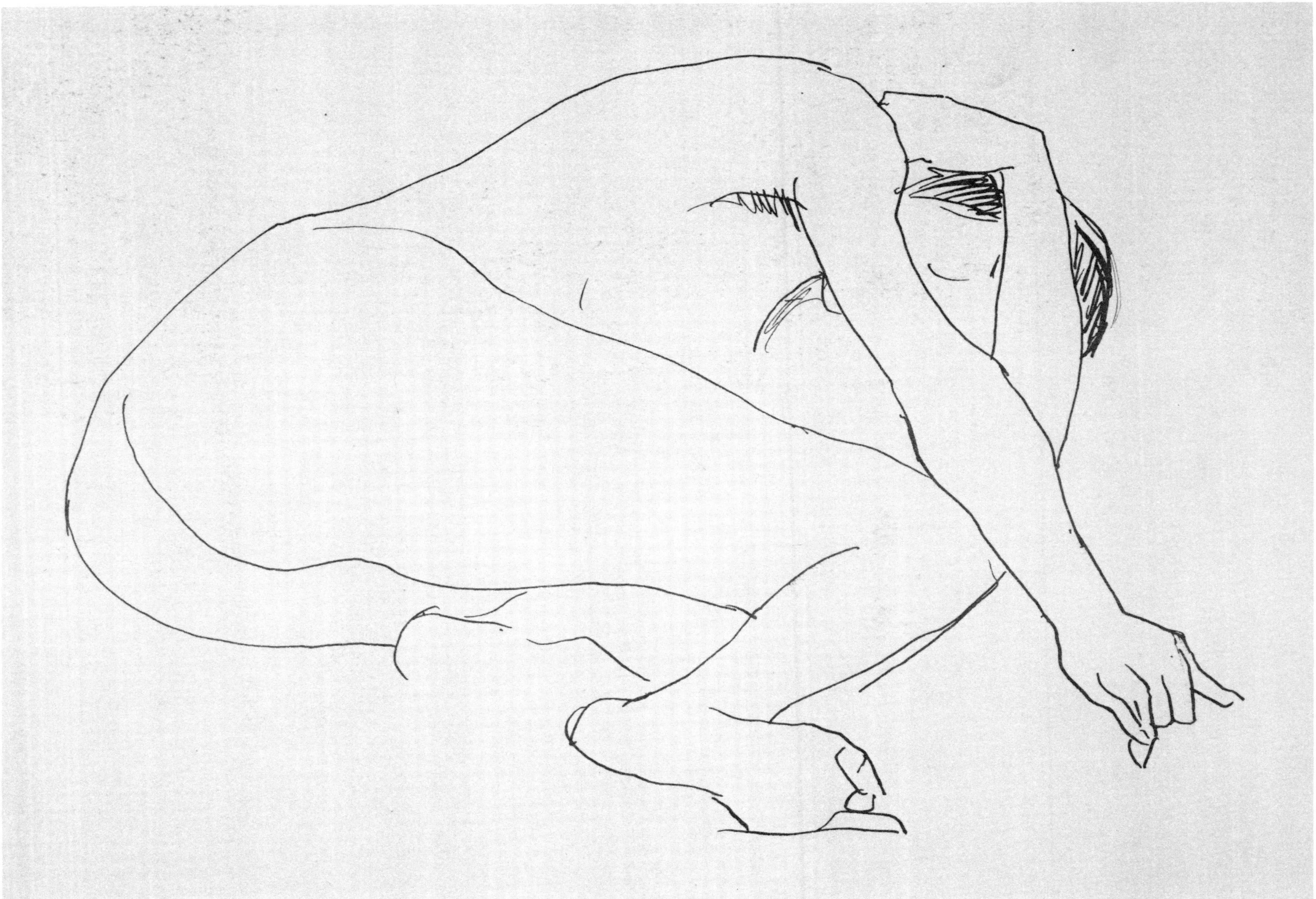

Reclining Nude, c. 1923–24
Ink on paper, 12⅞ × 15⅞ inches. Josephine N. Hopper Bequest 70.531 verso

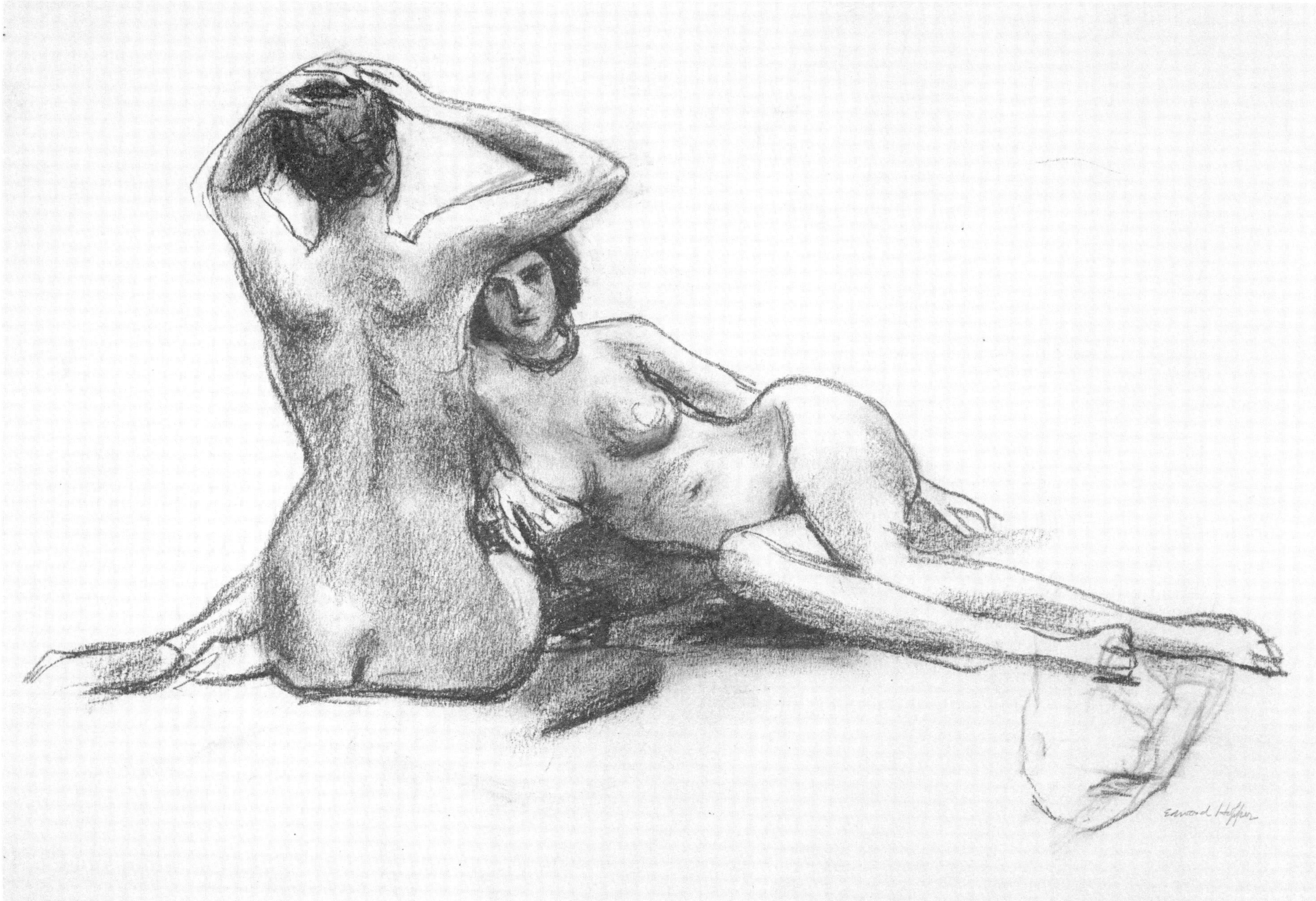

Two Nudes, Seated and Reclining, c. 1923–24
Sanguine on paper, 15$^{1}/_{16}$ × 22$^{1}/_{16}$ inches. Josephine N. Hopper Bequest 70.708

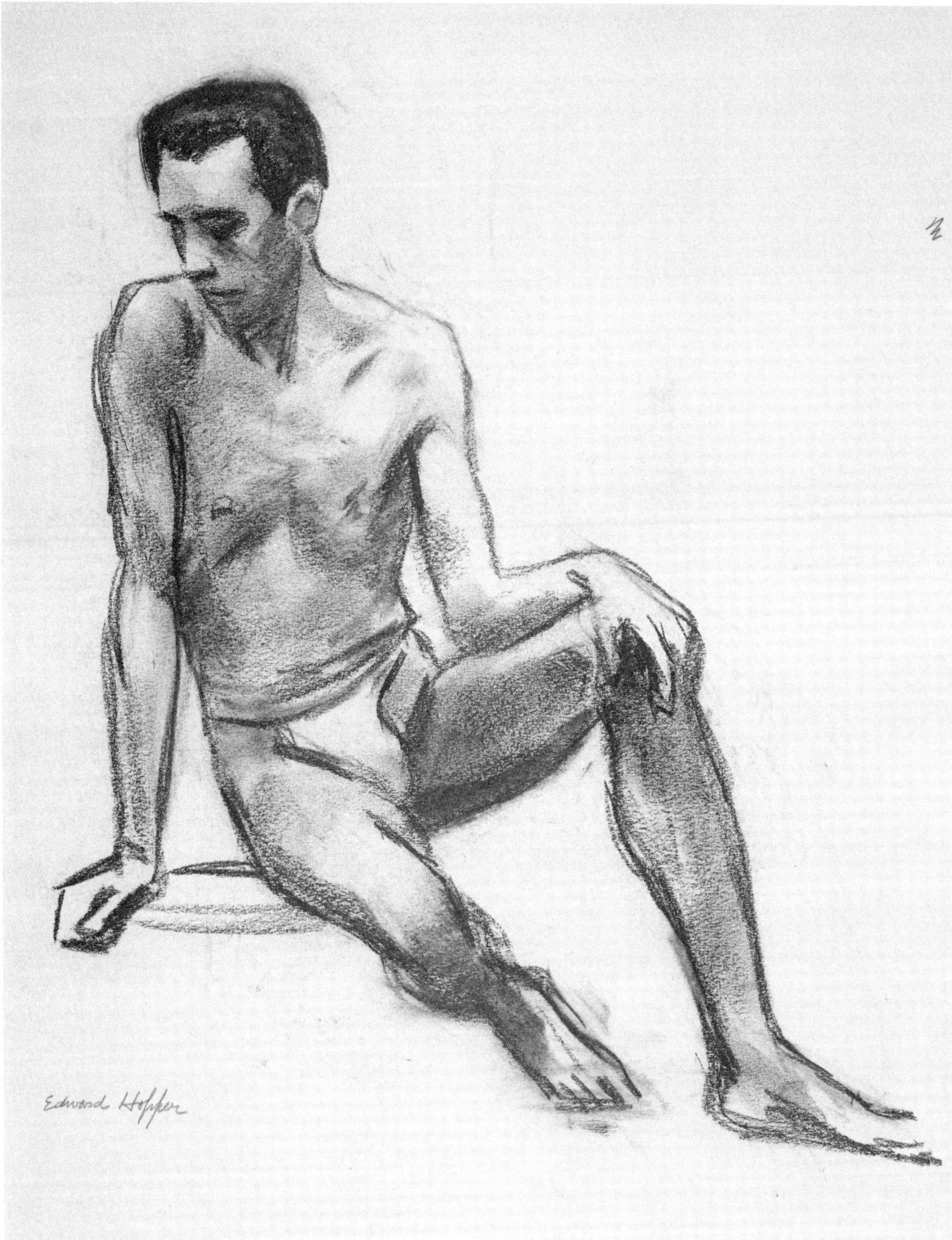

Seated Male Nude, c. 1923–24
Conté on paper, 22 × 15⅜ inches. Josephine N. Hopper Bequest 70.693

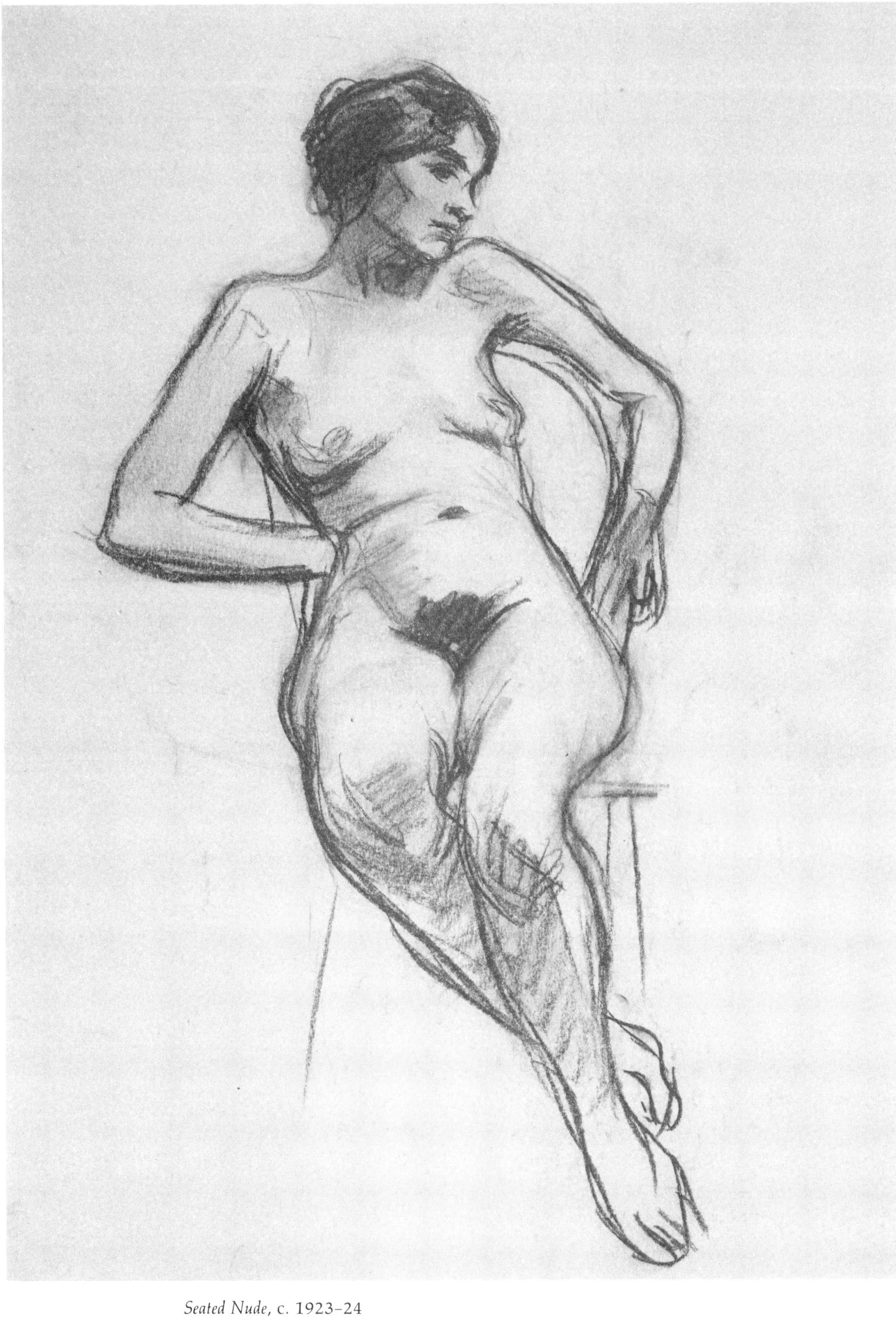

Seated Nude, c. 1923–24
Sanguine on paper, 14 × 10 inches. Josephine N. Hopper Bequest 70.562

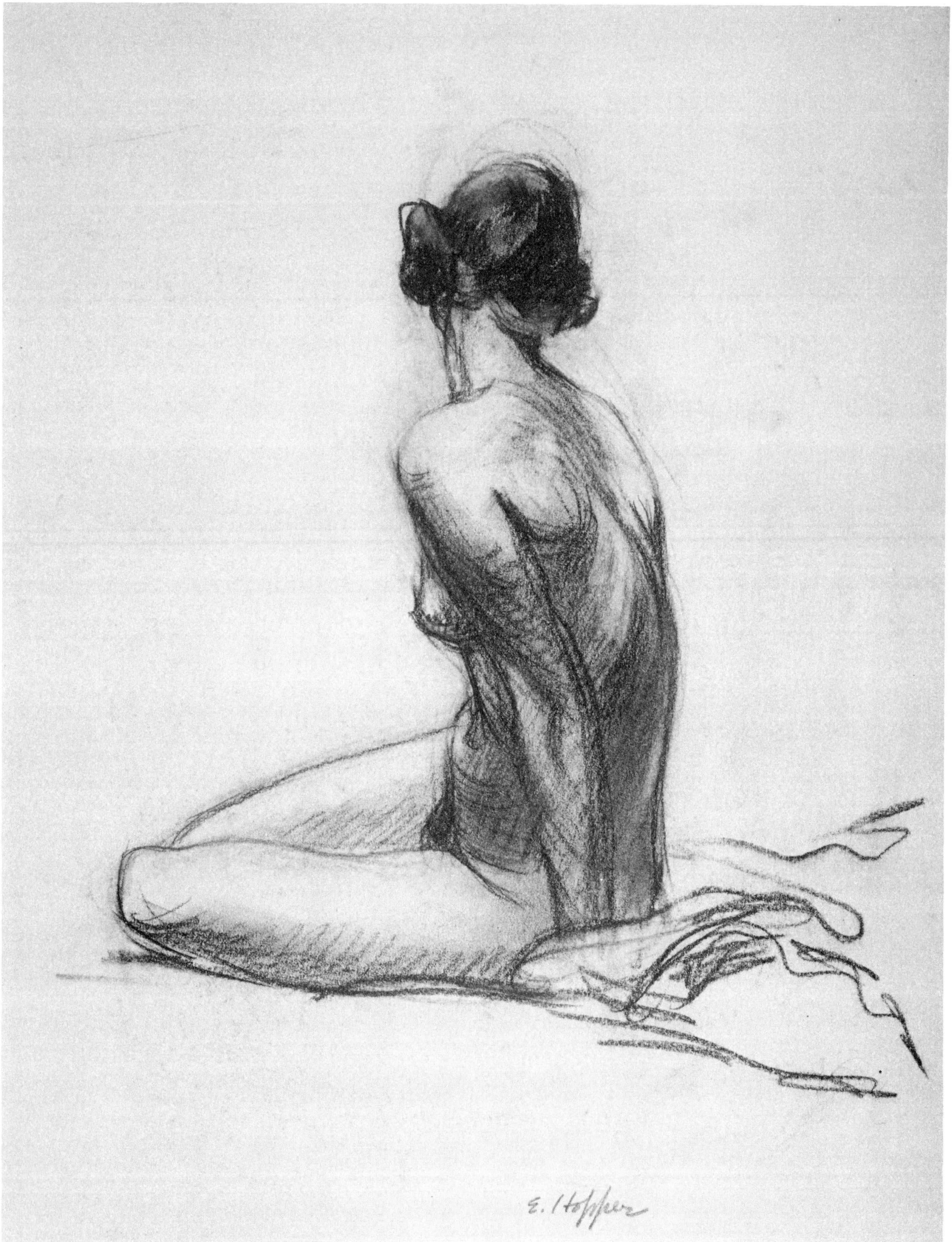

Seated Nude, c. 1923–24
Conté on paper, 16½ × 10⅝ inches. Josephine N. Hopper Bequest 70.403

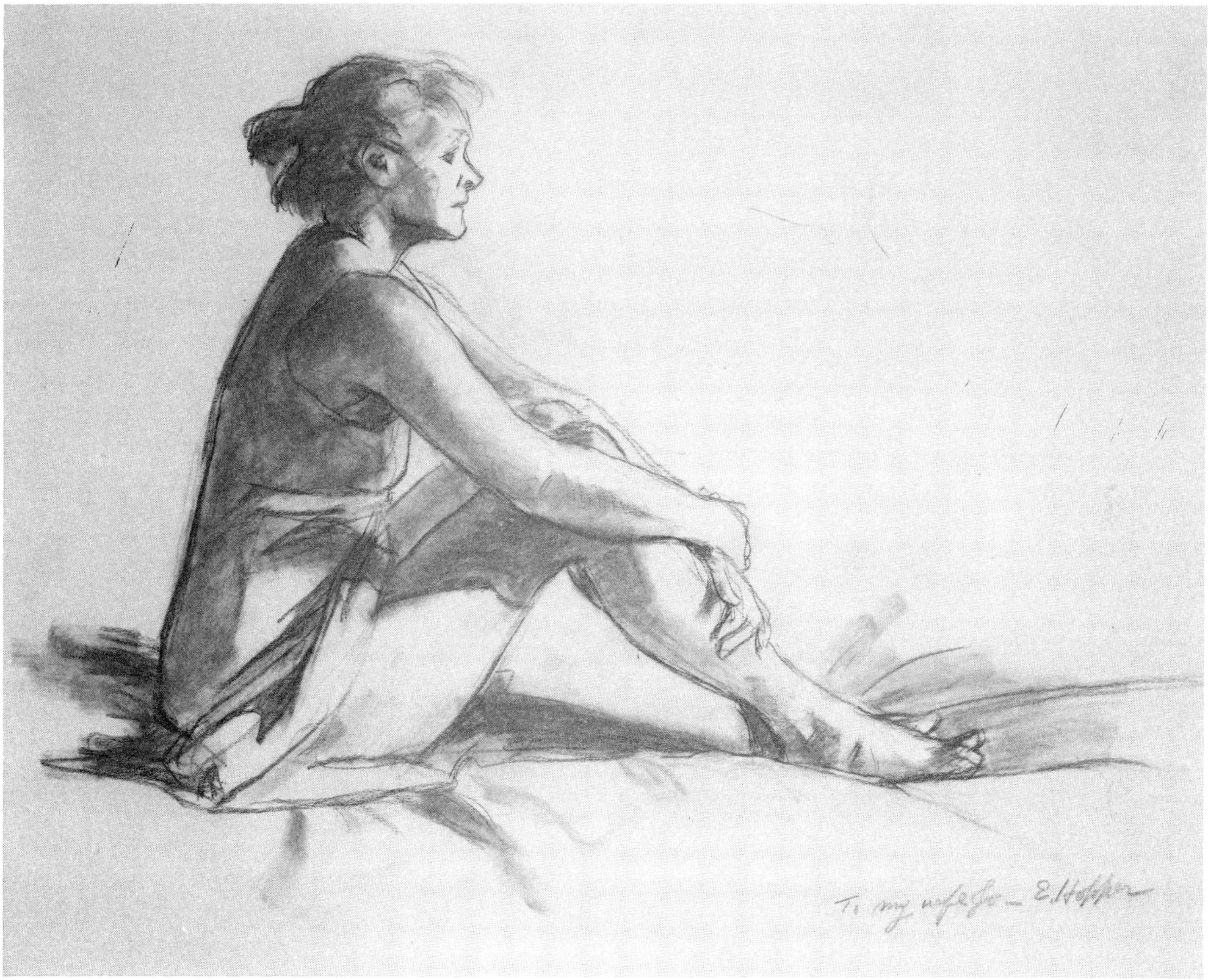

Study for *Morning Sun*, 1952
Conté on paper, 12 × 19 inches. Josephine N. Hopper Bequest 70.290

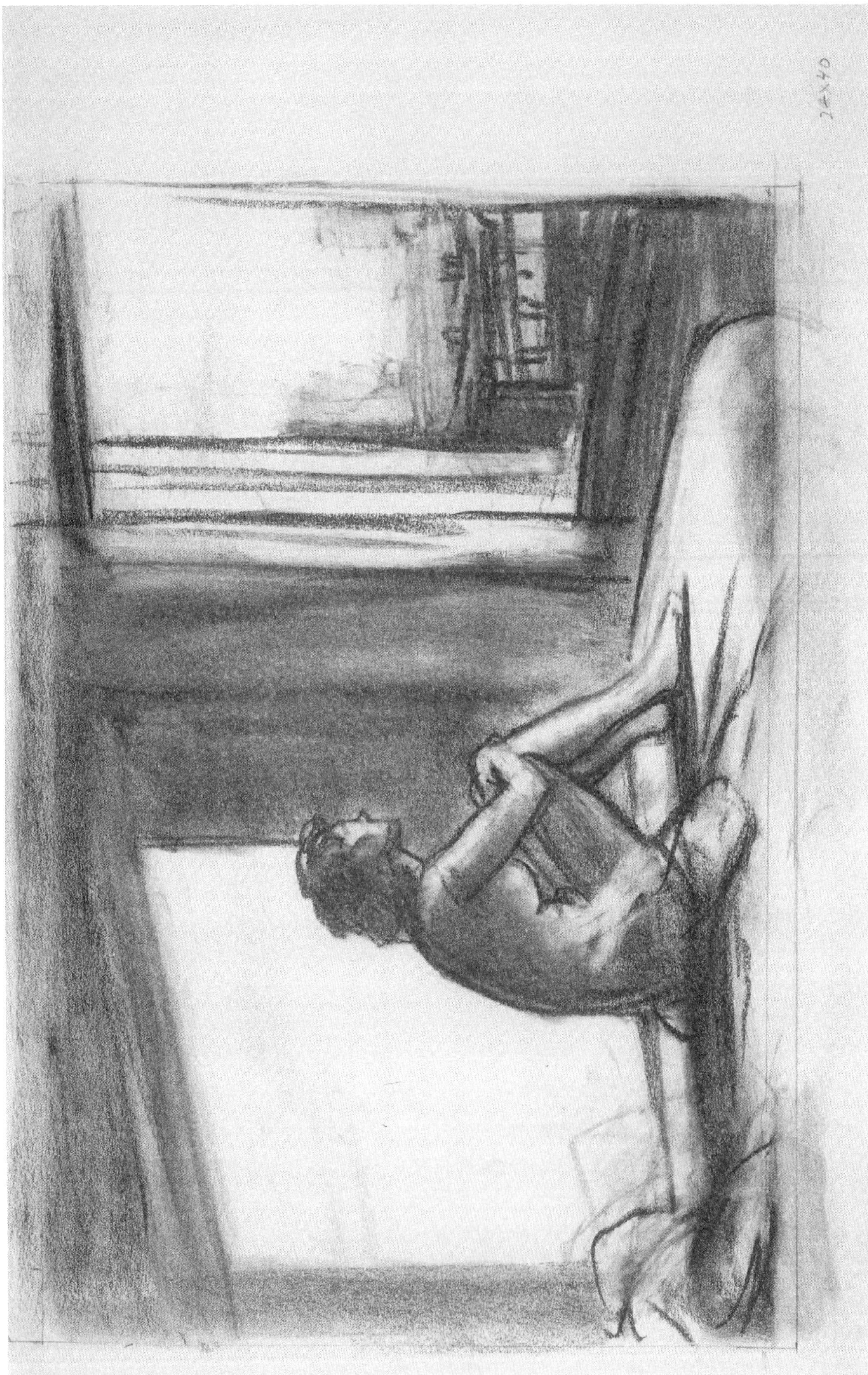

Study for *Morning Sun*, 1952
Conté on paper, 12 × 19 inches. Josephine N. Hopper Bequest 70.244

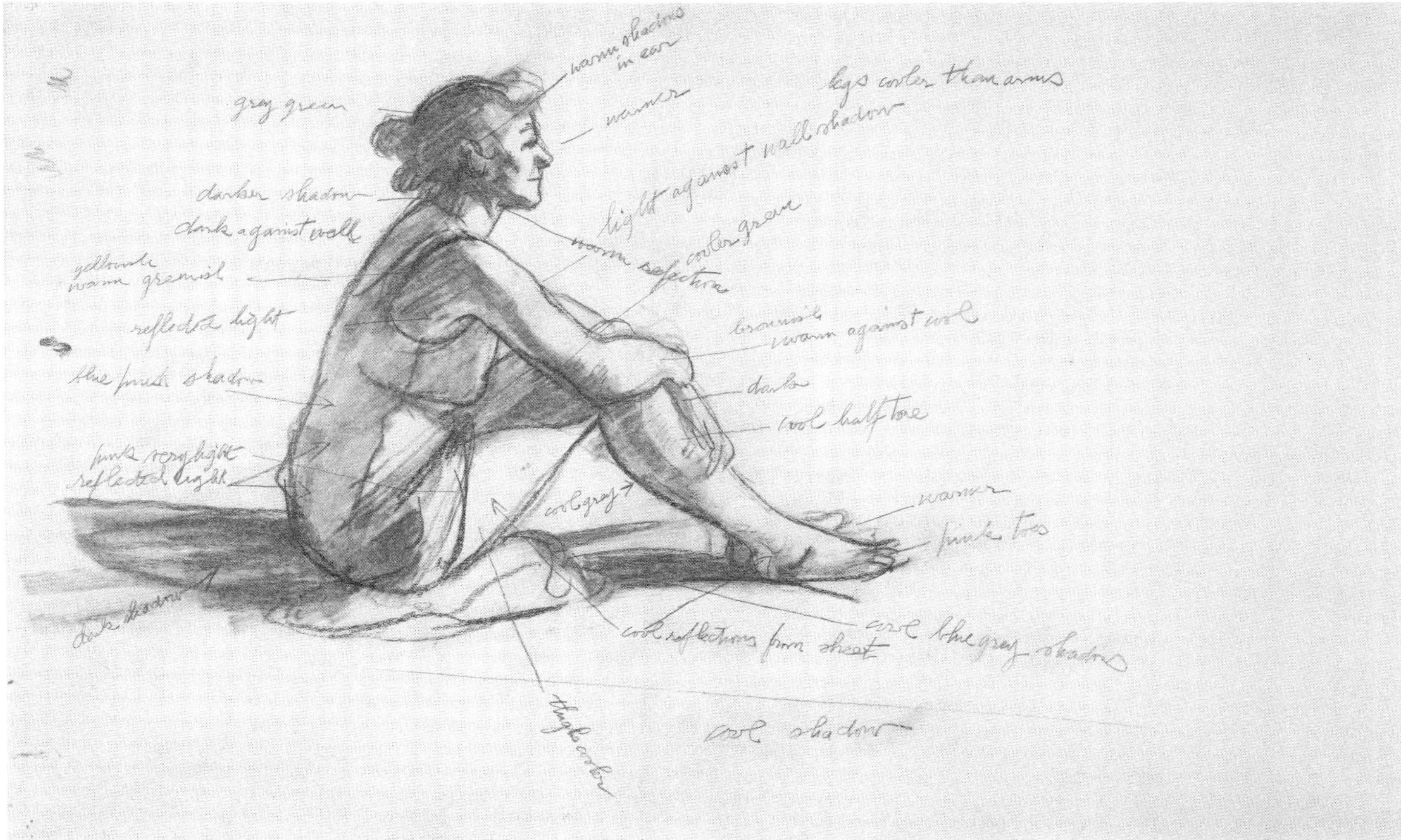

Study for *Morning Sun*, 1952
Conté on paper, 12 × 18 15/16 inches. Josephine N. Hopper Bequest 70.291

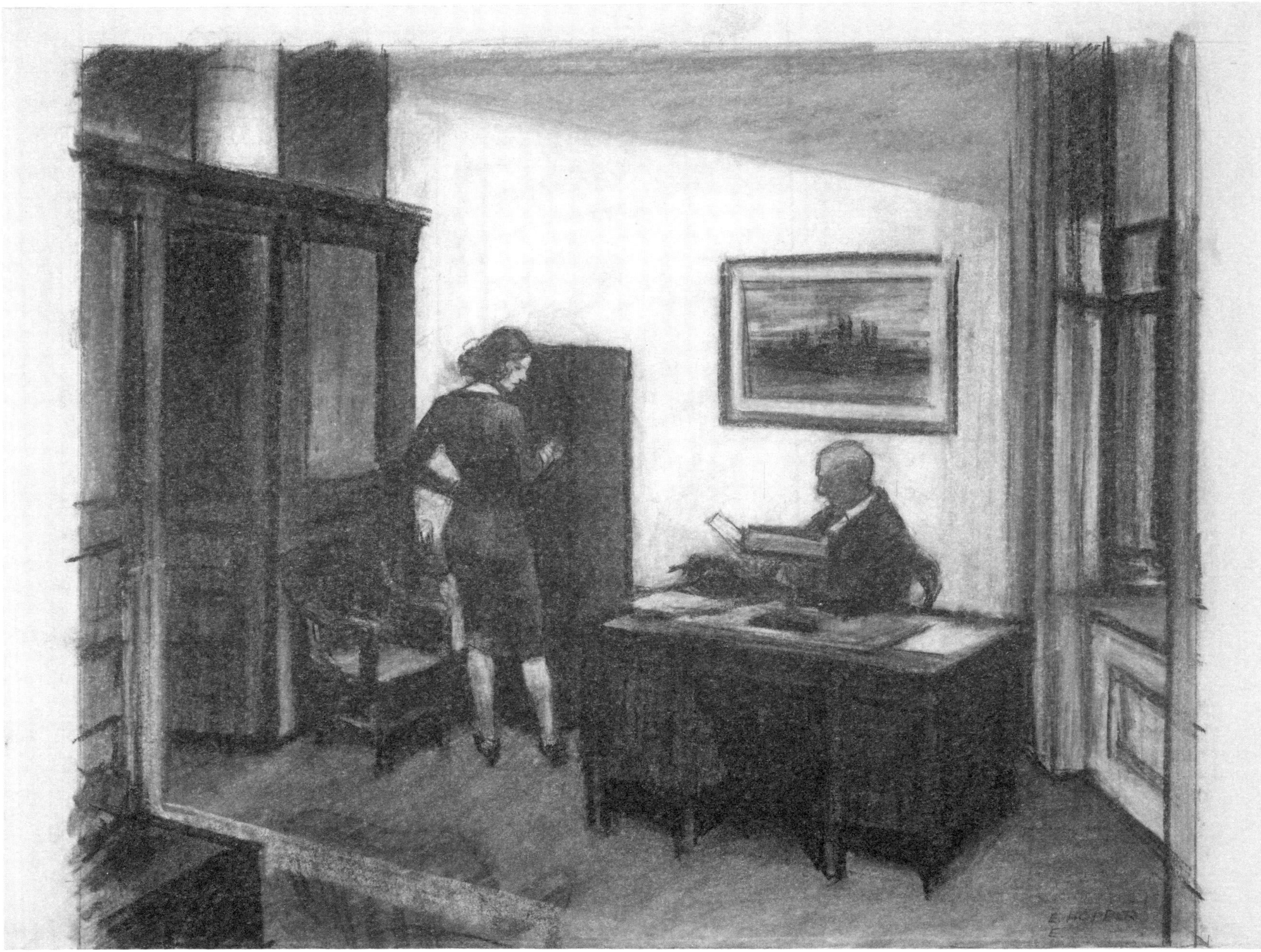

Study for *Office at Night*, 1940
Conté and charcoal with touches of white paint on paper, 15 × 19⅝ inches.
Josephine N. Hopper Bequest 70.340

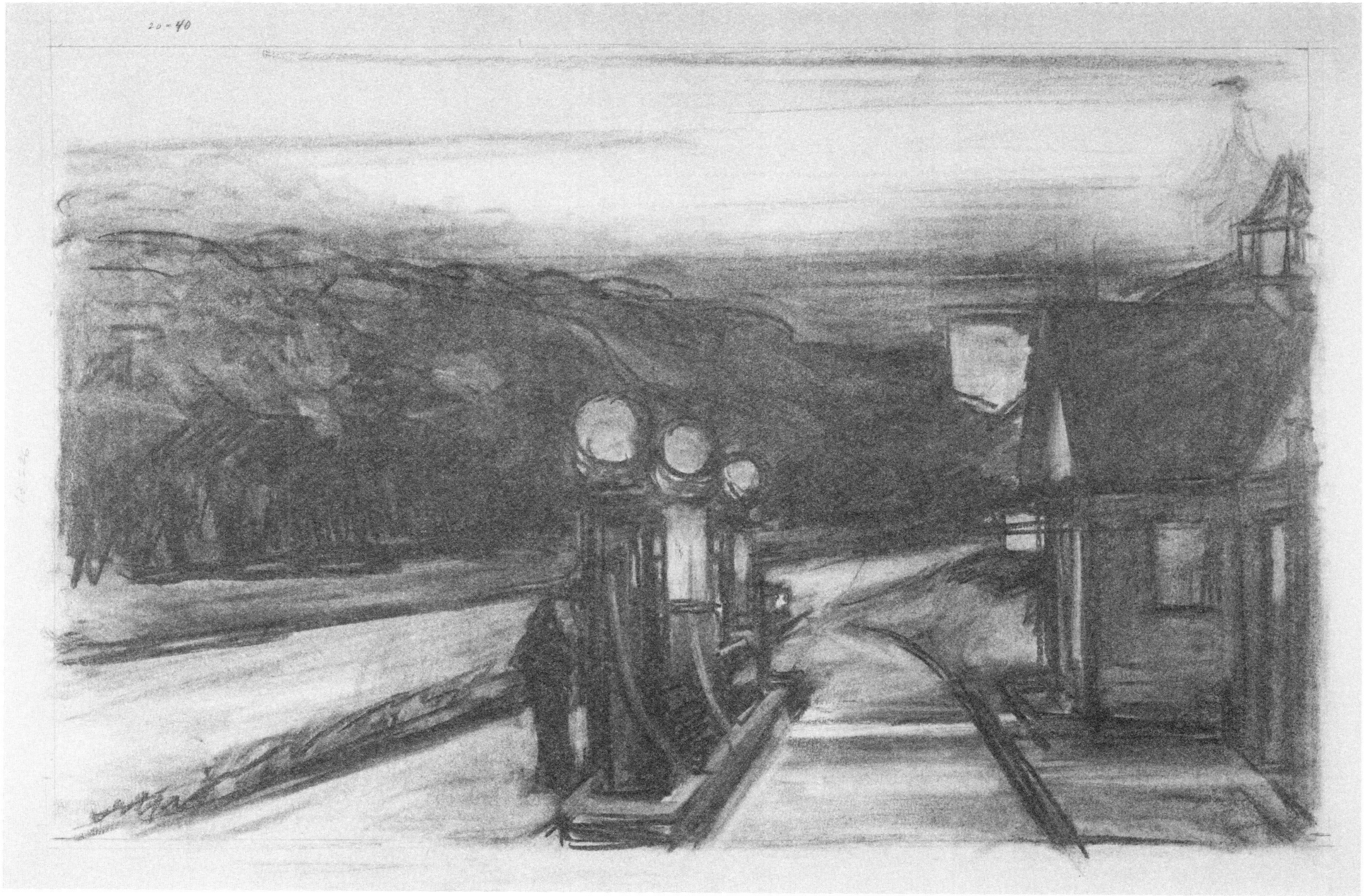

Study for *Gas*, 1940
Conté and pencil on paper, $15\frac{1}{16} \times 22\frac{1}{16}$ inches.
Josephine N. Hopper Bequest 70.300

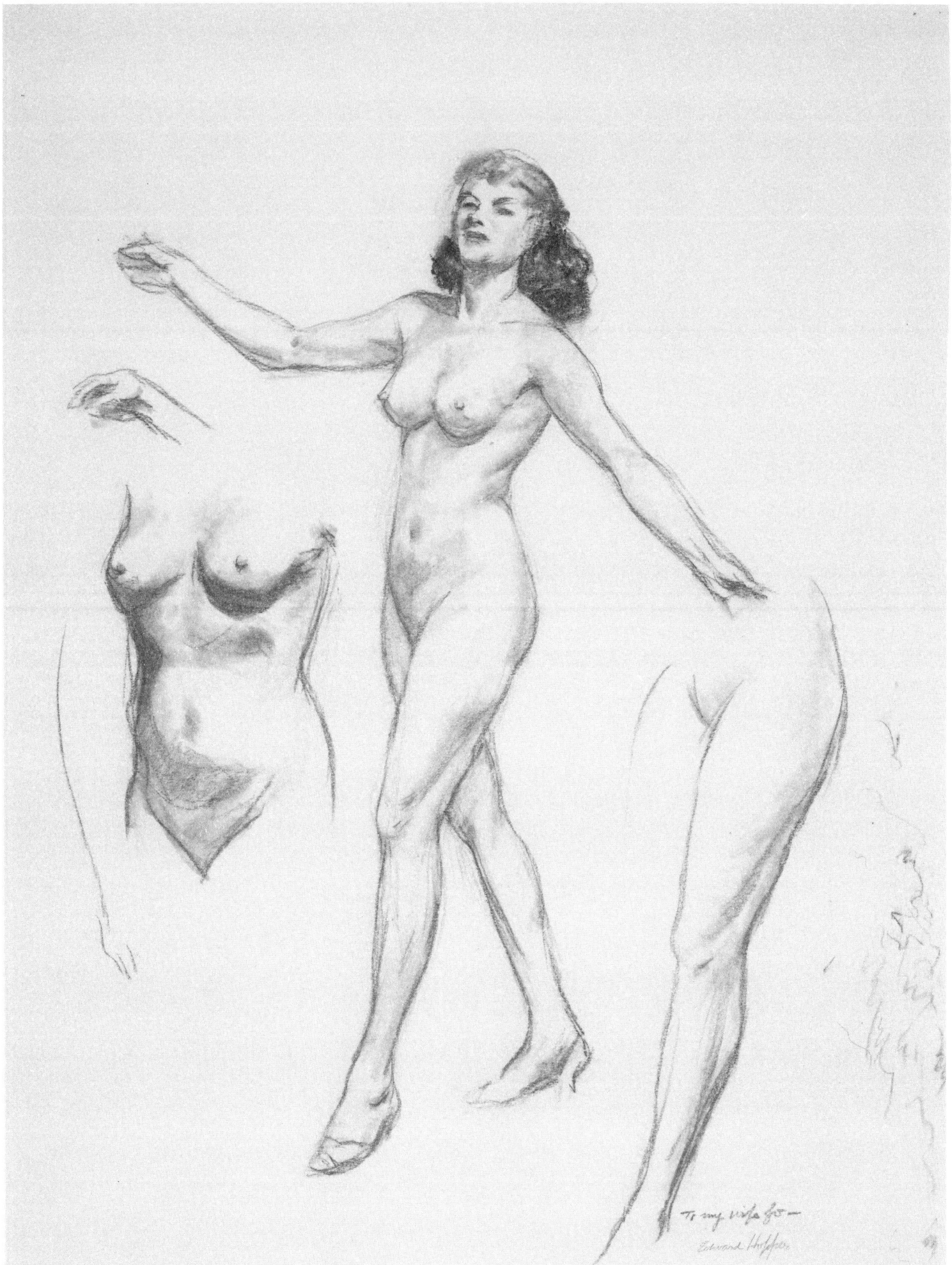

Study for *Girlie Show*, 1941
Conté on paper, 22⅛ × 15$^{1}/_{16}$ inches. Josephine N. Hopper Bequest 70.301

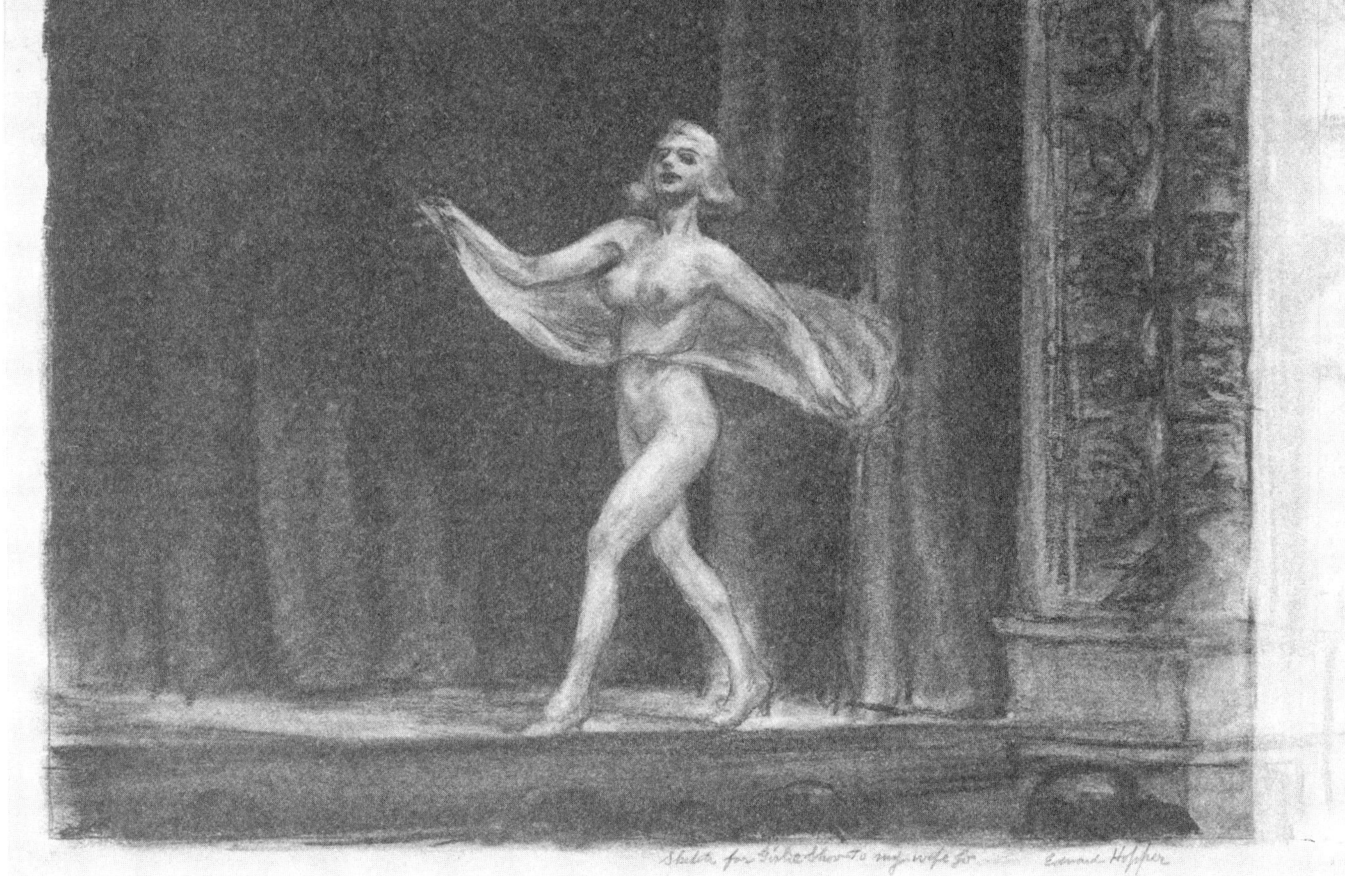

Study for *Girlie Show*, 1941
Conté on paper, 13¼ × 15 inches. Josephine N. Hopper Bequest 70.295

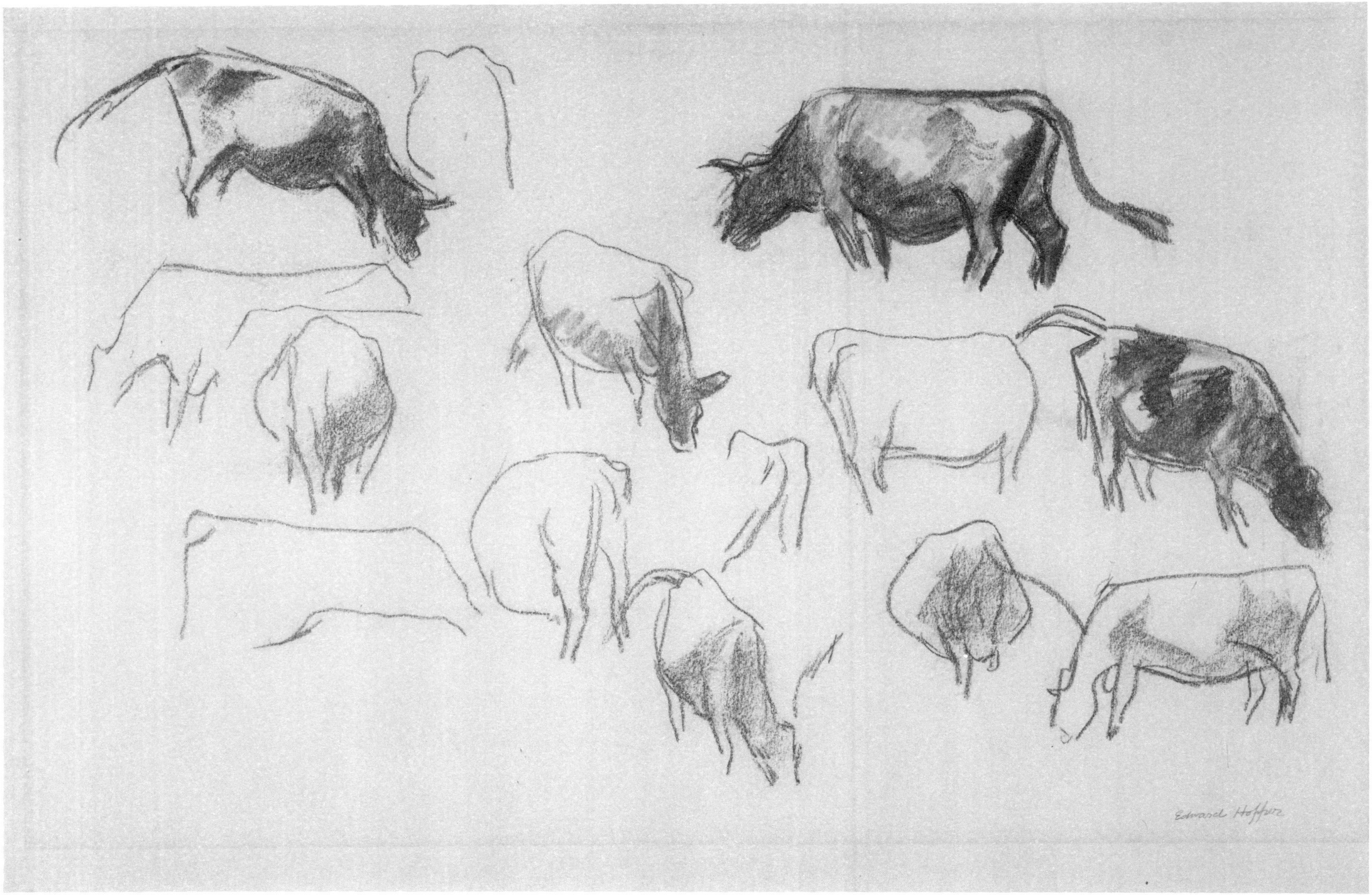

Studies of Cows, c. 1924–30
Conté on paper, 13½ × 21½ inches. Gift of Lucille and Walter Fillin 75.20

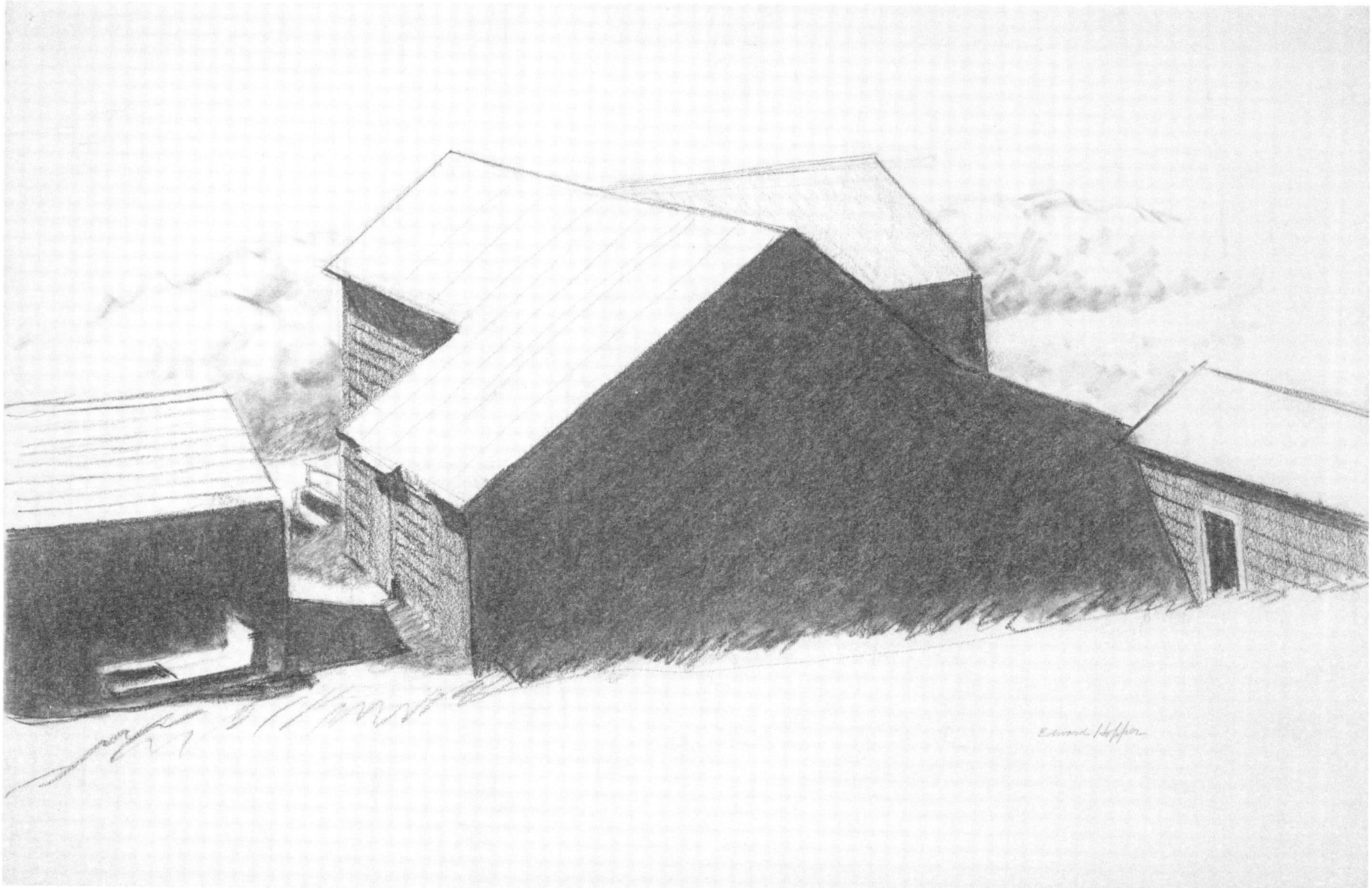

Cobb's Barns, South Truro, c. 1931
Conté and red crayon on paper, 15 × 22⅛ inches.
Josephine N. Hopper Bequest 70.684

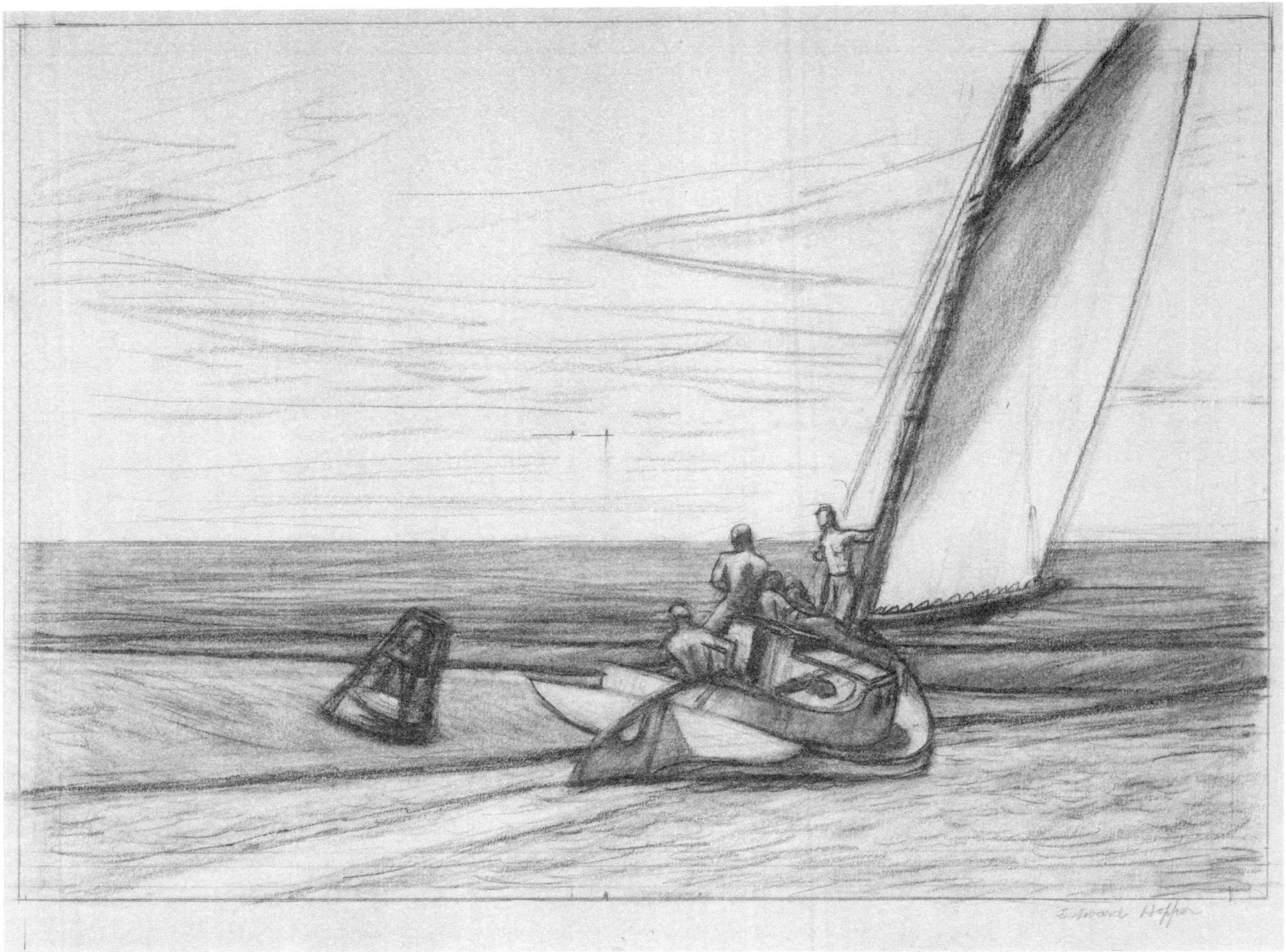

Study for *Ground Swell*, 1939
Conté and charcoal on paper, 15 × 22 inches.
Josephine N. Hopper Bequest 70.339

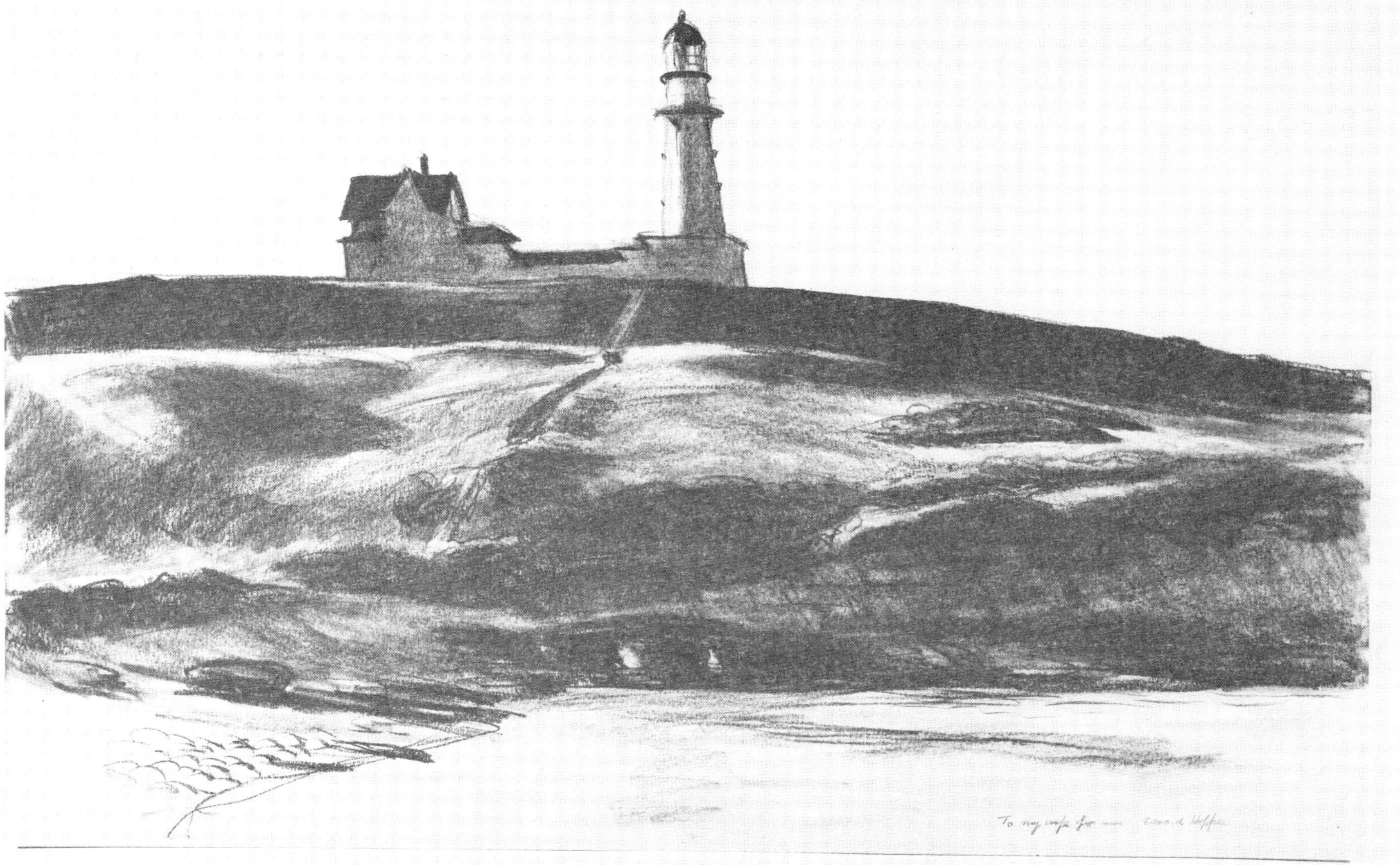

Light at Two Lights (study for *Lighthouse Hill*), 1927
Conté and charcoal on paper, 15 × 22$^{1}/_{16}$ inches.
Josephine N. Hopper Bequest 70.683

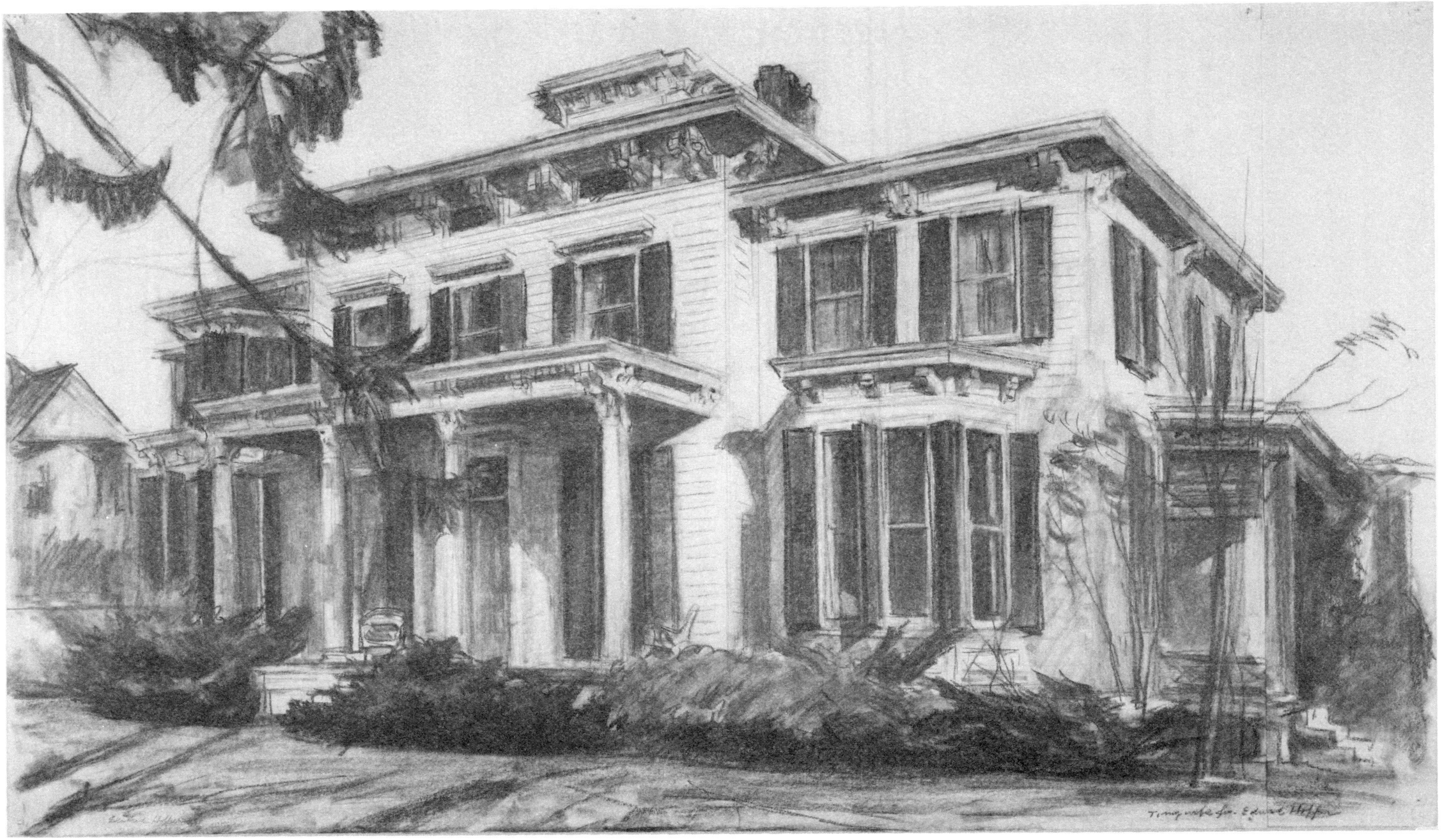

Study for *Pretty Penny*, 1939
Conté on paper, 15 1/16 × 25 1/16 inches. Josephine N. Hopper Bequest 70.658

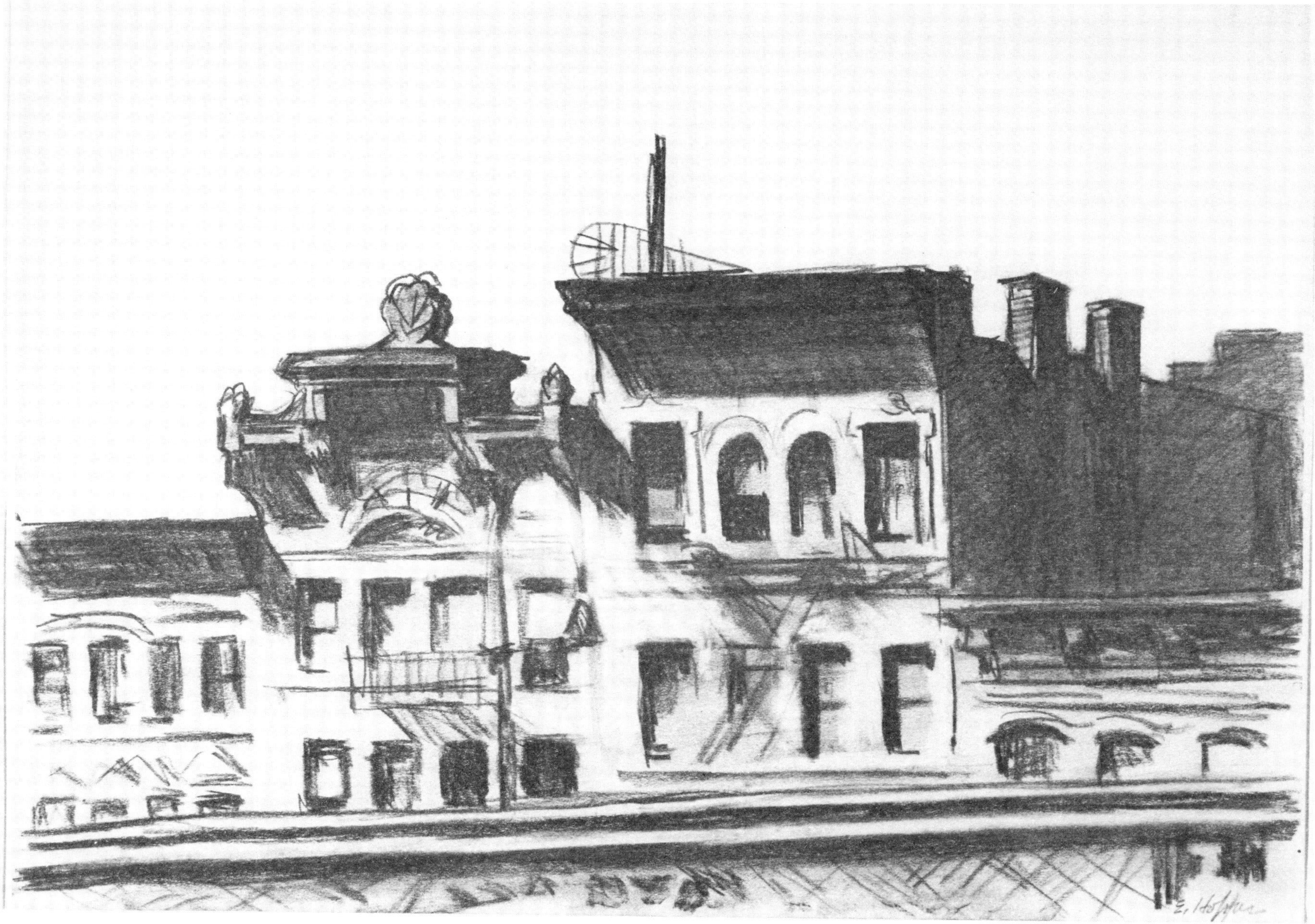

Study for *From Williamsburg Bridge*, 1928
Conté on paper, $8\frac{1}{2} \times 11\frac{1}{16}$ inches. Josephine N. Hopper Bequest 70.457

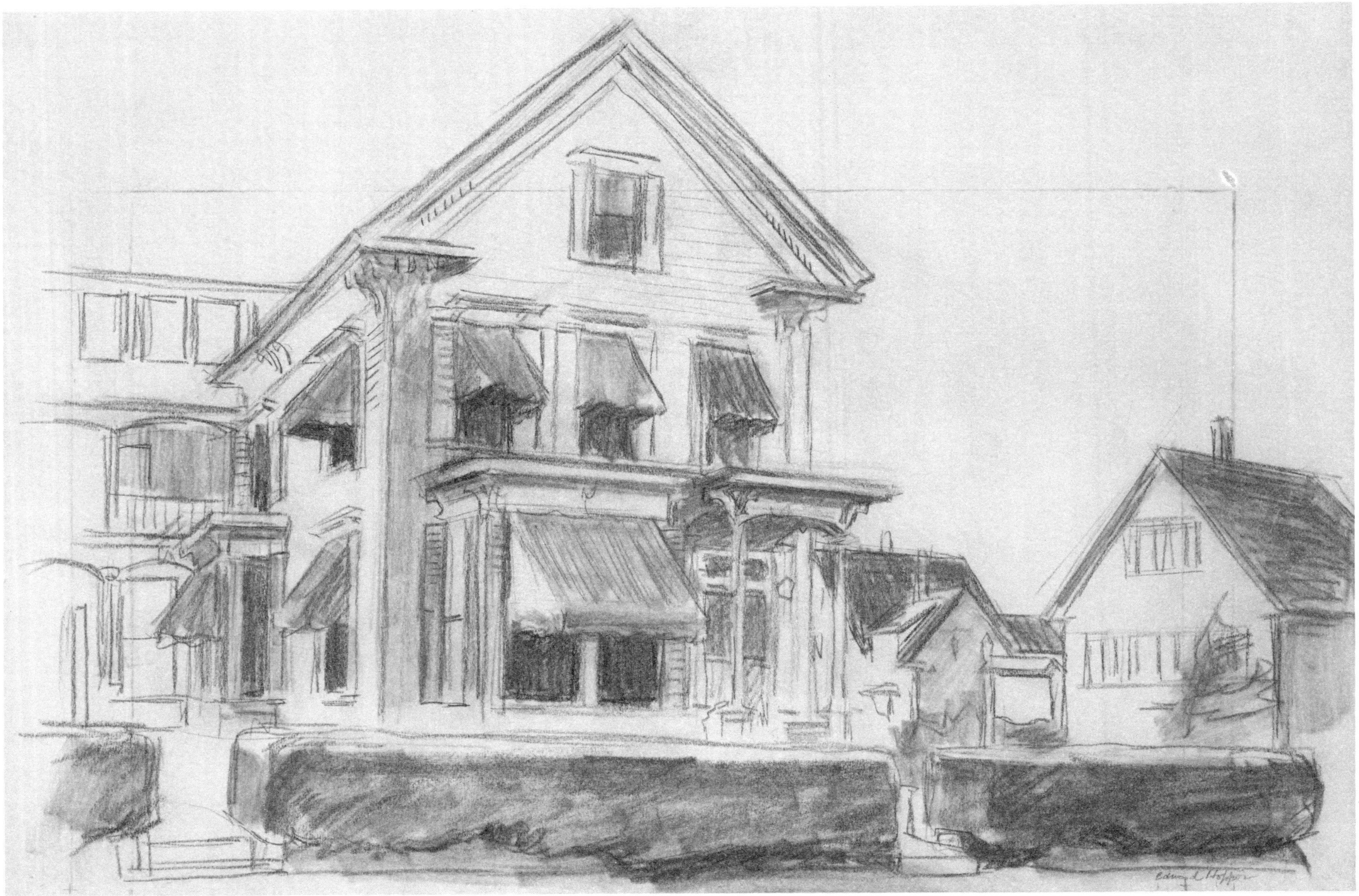

Study for *Rooms for Tourists*, 1945
Conté on paper, 15 × 22¼ inches. Josephine N. Hopper Bequest 70.848

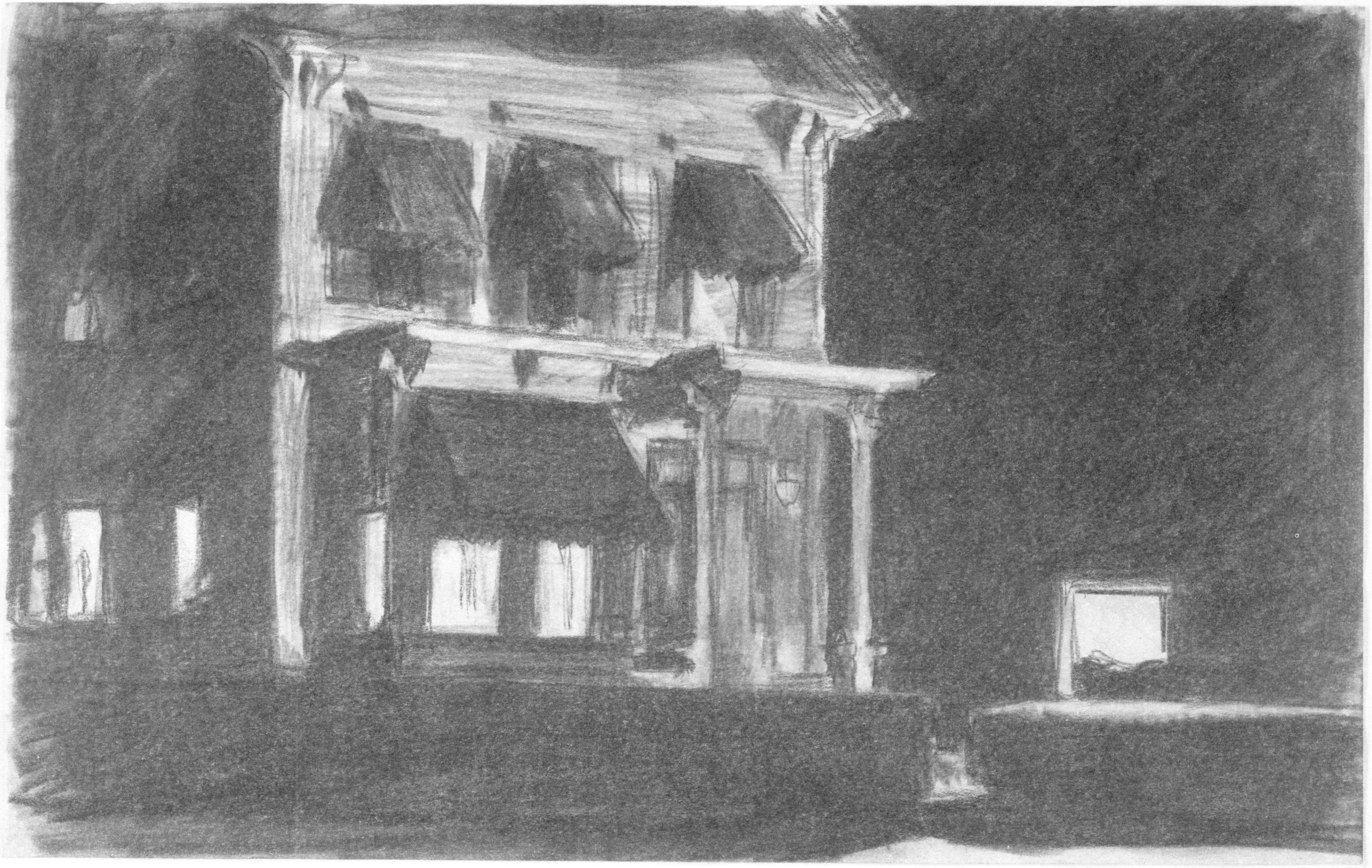

Study for *Rooms for Tourists*, 1945
Conté and charcoal on paper, $10\frac{3}{8} \times 16$ inches.
Josephine N. Hopper Bequest   70.438

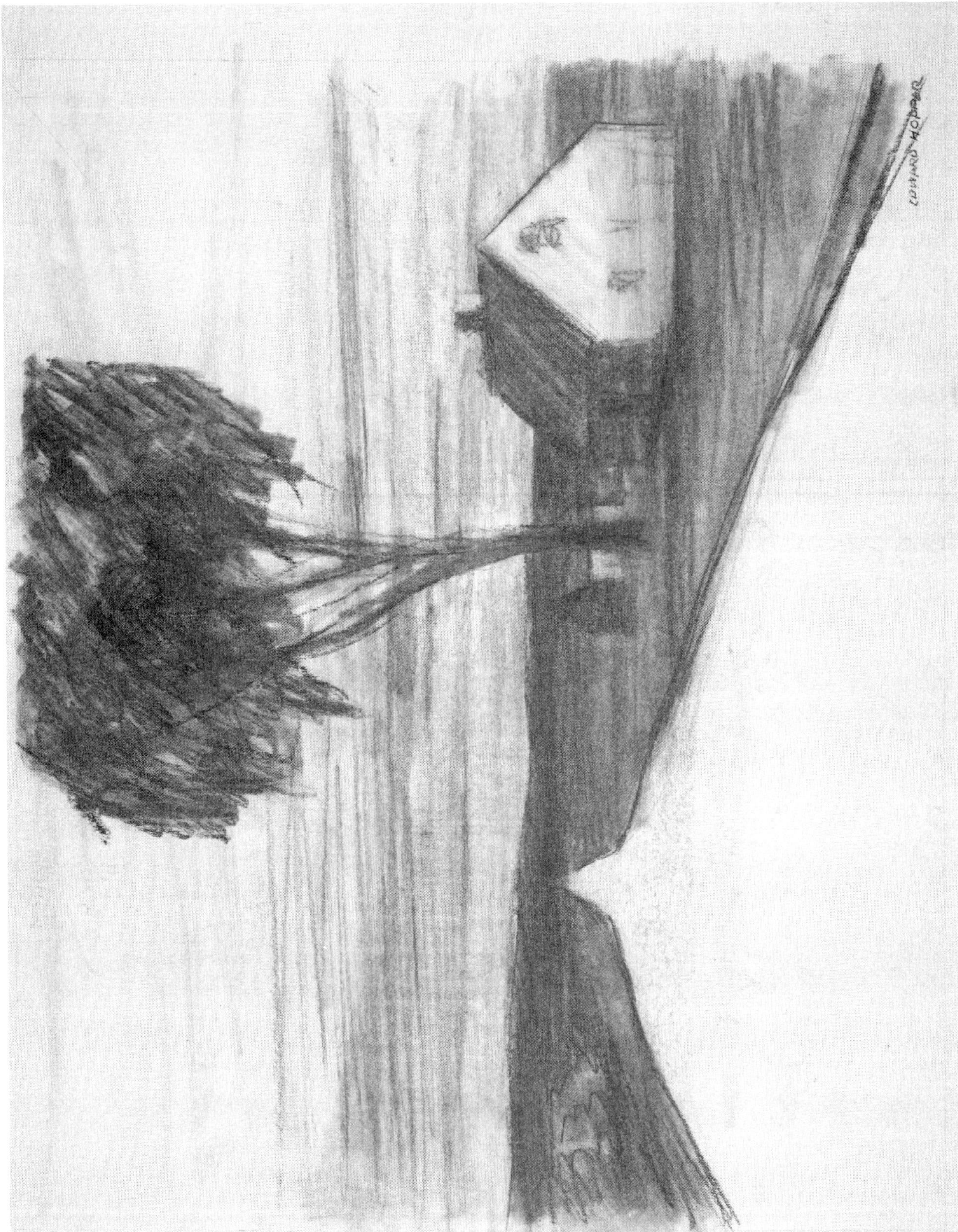

Study for *Solitude*, 1944
Conté and sanguine on paper, 15 × 18 inches.
Josephine N. Hopper Bequest 70.685

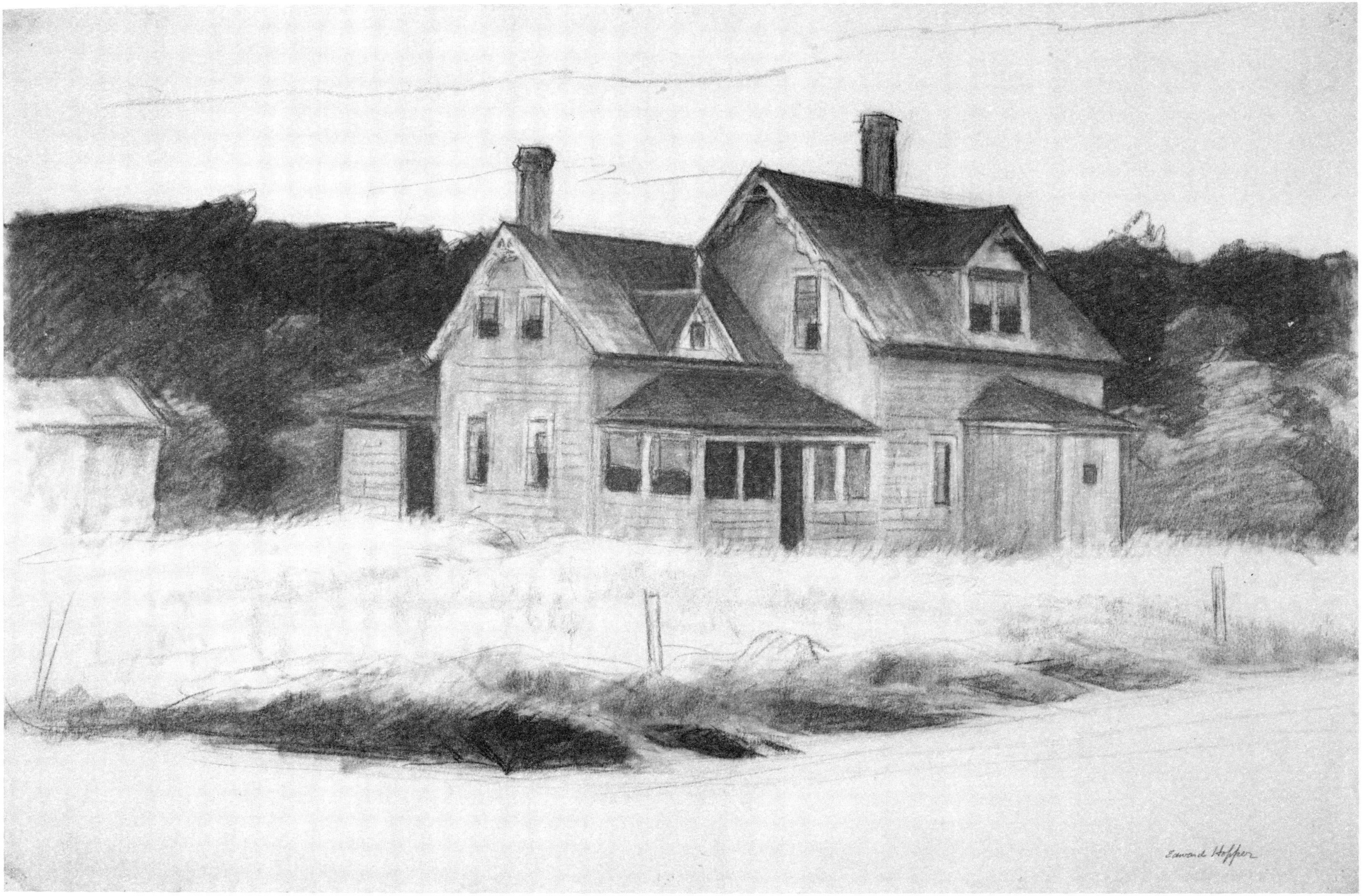

Study for *House by a Road*, 1940
Conté on paper, 10½ × 16 inches. Josephine N. Hopper Bequest 70.673

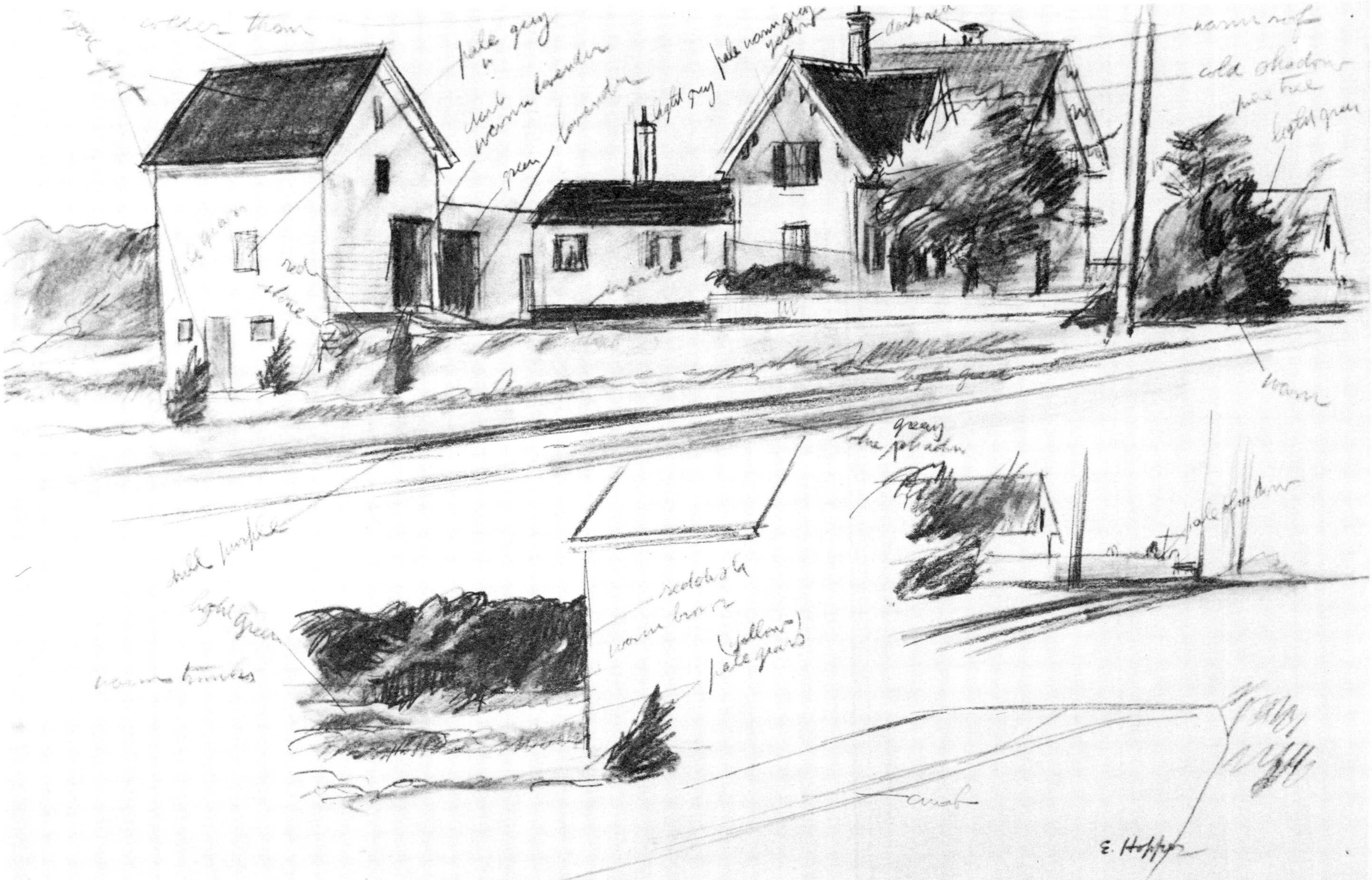

Study for *Route 6, Eastham*, 1941
Conté on paper, 10½ × 16 inches. Josephine N. Hopper Bequest 70.330

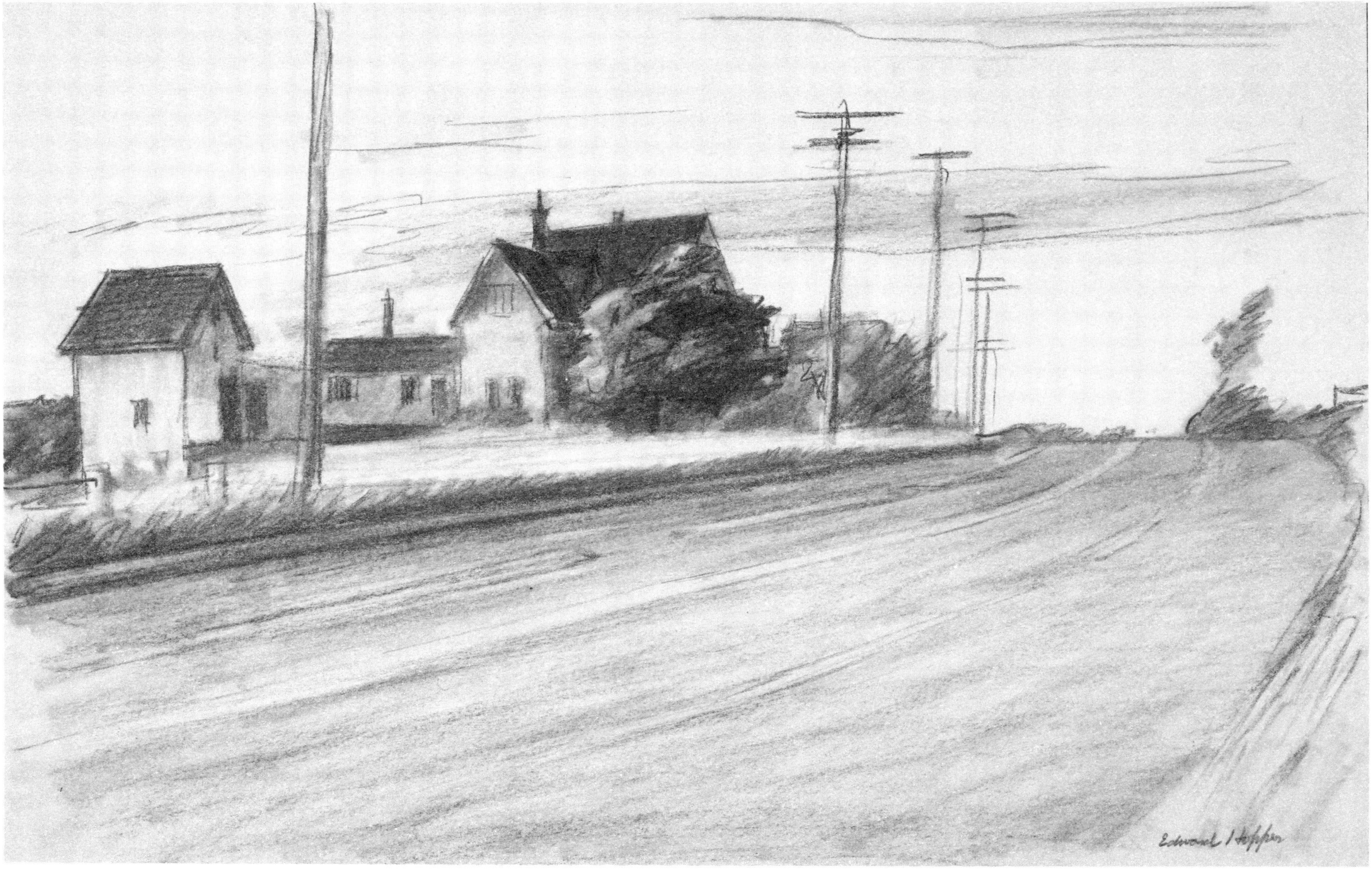

Study for *Route 6, Eastham,* 1941
Conté on paper, 10⅝ × 16 inches. Josephine N. Hopper Bequest 70.446

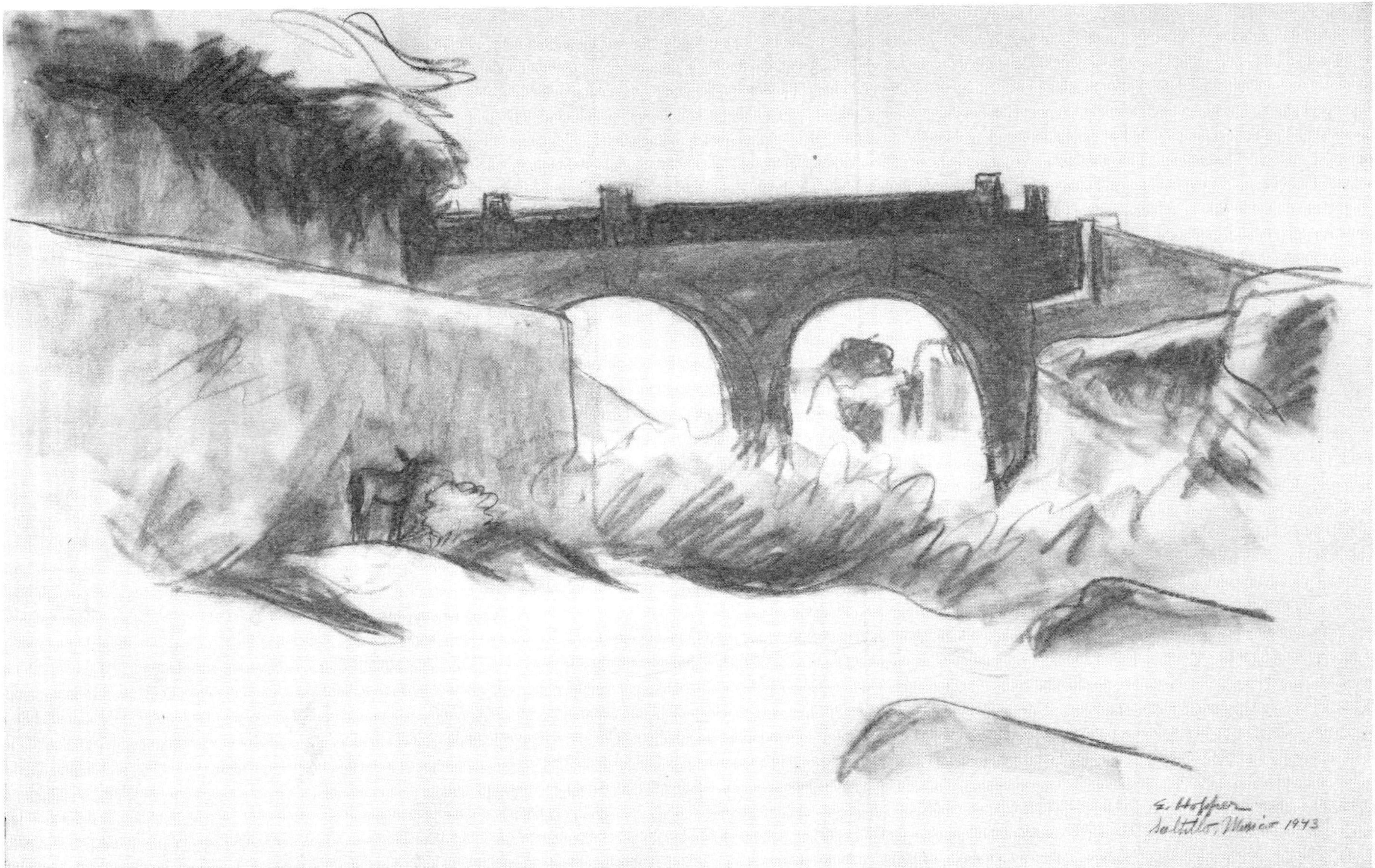

Saltillo, Mexico, 1943
Conté on paper, 10½ × 16 inches. Josephine N. Hopper Bequest 70.651

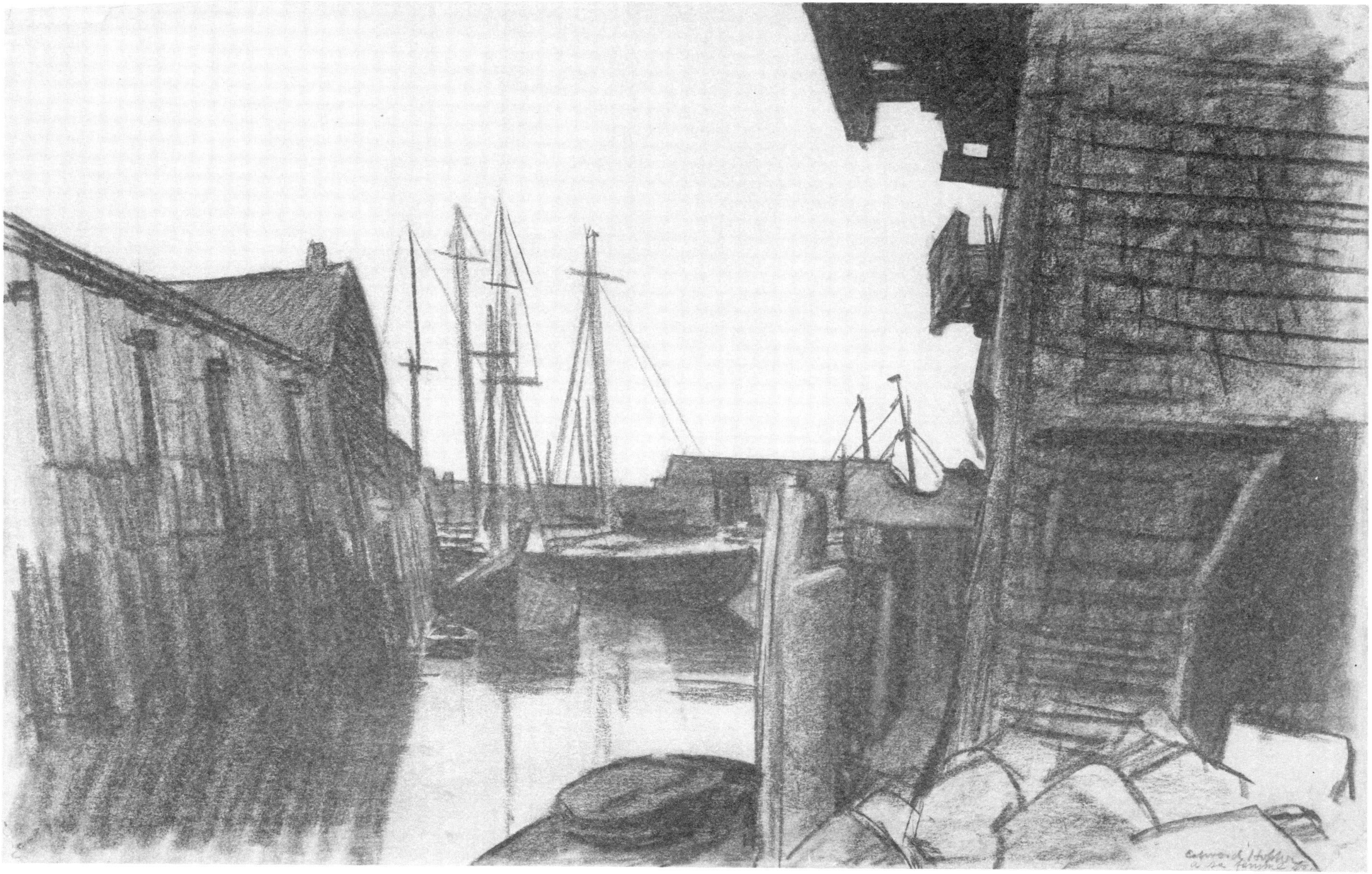

Docks and Boats, n.d.
Conté and charcoal on paper, $11^{13}/_{16} \times 18^{1}/_{16}$ inches.
Josephine N. Hopper Bequest 70.304

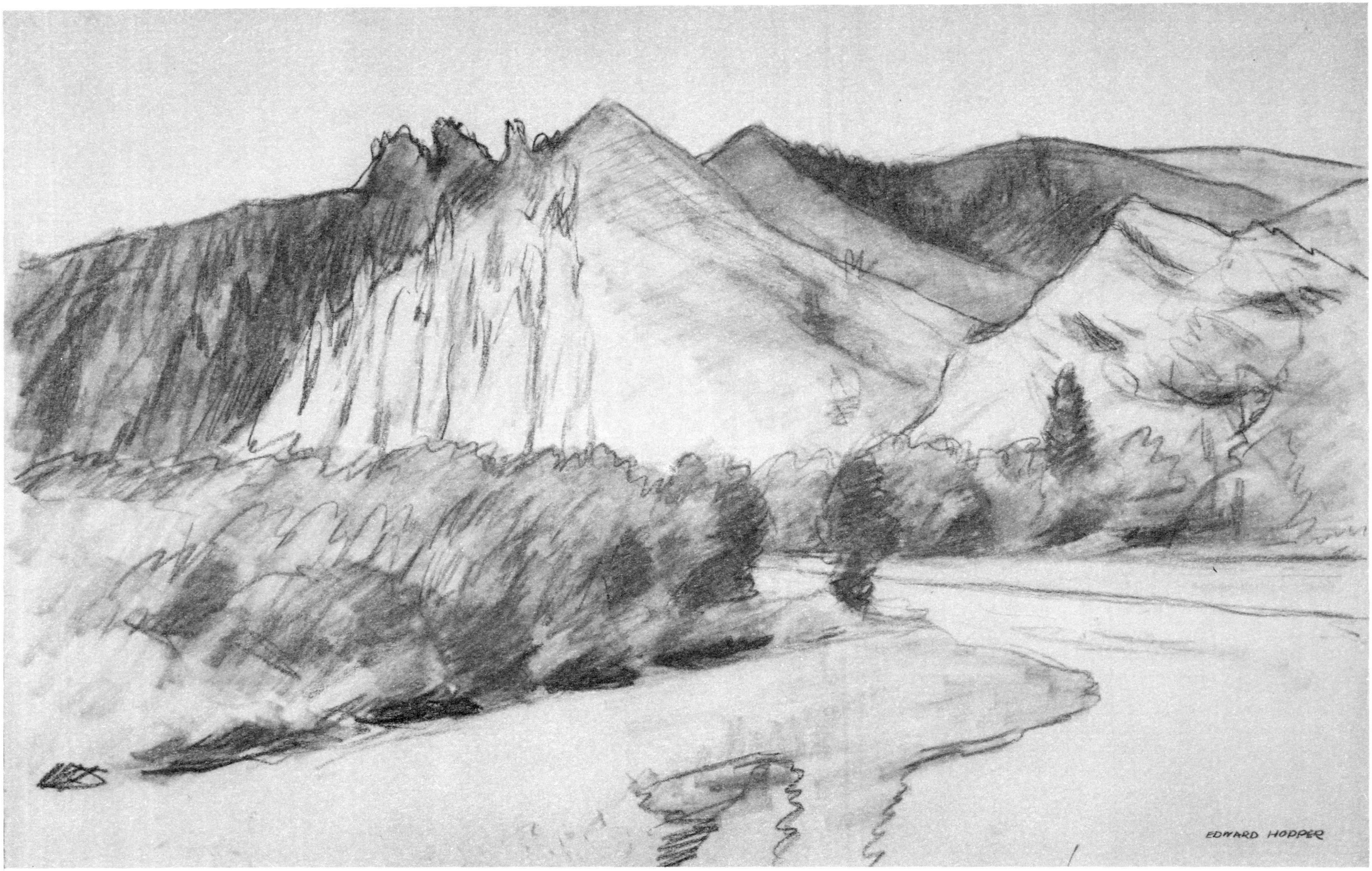

River and Mountains, n.d.
Conté on paper, 10¾ × 16 inches. Josephine N. Hopper Bequest 70.365

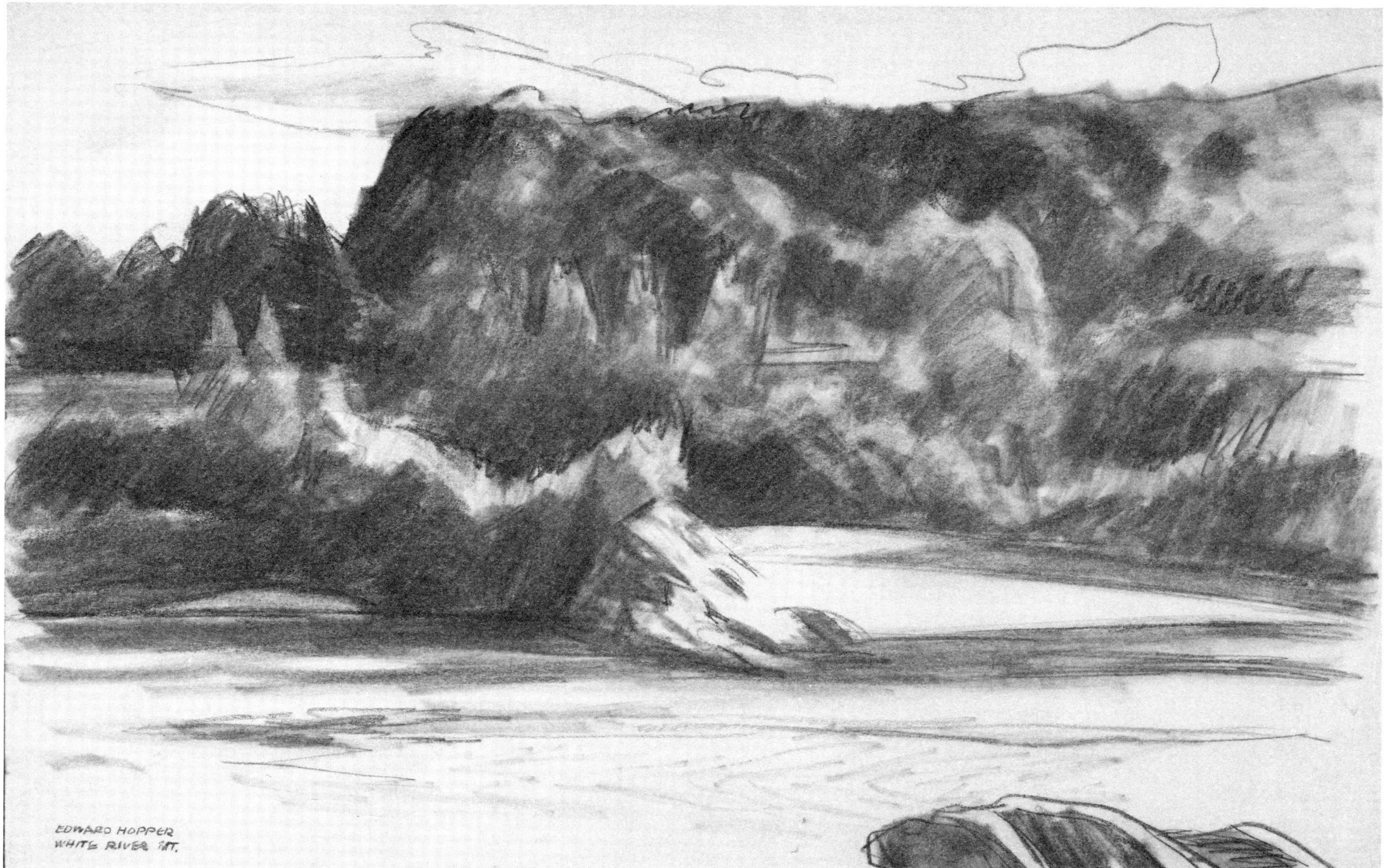

White River, Vermont, 1937–38
Conté on paper, 10½ × 16 inches. Josephine N. Hopper Bequest 70.372

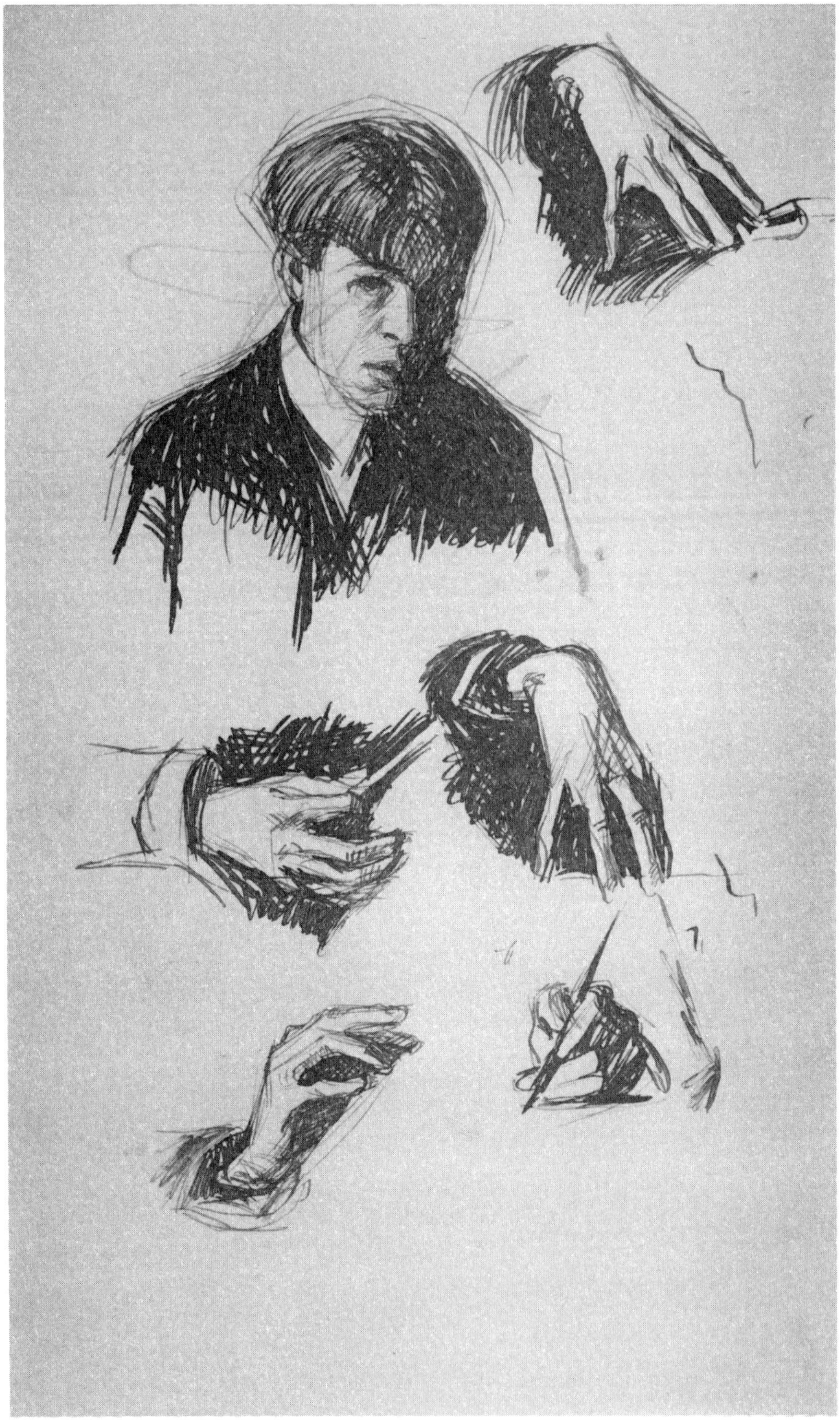

Self-Portrait and Hand Studies, c. 1900
Ink on paper, 7⅞ × 5 inches. Josephine N. Hopper Bequest 70.1559.28